LORDS OF SPEED

The Great Drivers of Formula 1

BY
ROBERTO GURIAN

SCHIFFER
PUBLISHING
4880 Lower Valley Road • Atglen, PA 19310

8

contents

Previous pages: The driving style of Alberto Ascari in his Ferrari 125 F1 at Silverstone in 1949. The Italian driver was a two-time World Champion and the only rival Juan Manuel Fangio truly feared.

foreword

They have been called the knights of risk. Fearless heroes who staked their lives every time they sat behind the wheel, with just one goal: to drive as fast as possible and . . . win. While modern advancements have significantly reduced risks—and thankfully, severe accidents are rare—the allure of the racing driver remains as strong as ever. In the postwar era, British commentators often compared race car drivers to the RAF heroes who flew Spitfires to fend off German bombers during the famed Battle of Britain. Ironically, part of the British press criticized Jackie Stewart and Jochen Rindt in the late 1960s for their safety advocacy. Some believed that risk was a natural filter, separating the best drivers from the rest. But that "filter" came at a price: at least ten fatal crashes per season across all motorsport categories. It's no surprise that many of the drivers featured in this book are no longer with us—and, for most of them, their deaths were tied to accidents. However, our selection isn't based on their fates, the circumstances of their deaths, or even their career victories. Among the many who raced and risked it all, we chose those with the most profound human depth, those whose stories deserve to be told. Take Alfonso de Portago, for example, a Spanish aristocrat who lived a life straight out of a fairy tale, surrounded by women, horses, bobsleds, and roaring race cars. Naturally, we couldn't overlook the champions of recent generations, but the further back in time one goes, the more extraordinary and morally compelling these figures become. David Purley, for instance, won just a handful of Formula 3 races but proved himself a genuine hero. We chose him over others, including World Champions, whose stories lacked the same emotional impact. Our decision to highlight Piers Courage might surprise some readers. His tale illustrates the immense sacrifices required to follow one's passion—not just abandoning financial comfort but embracing the inherent risks of the sport. Beyond Formula 1—which didn't exist during their peak years—we also spotlight some of the greatest champions of earlier eras. Figures like Bernd Rosemeyer and, above all, Tazio Nuvolari stand out. Both were fearless, exceptionally talented heroes who captured the public's imagination. Rosemeyer's career lasted just three seasons, yet his impact on motorsport history is unforgettable. Nuvolari, on the other hand, enjoyed a long career filled with improbable feats, devastating crashes, and miraculous comebacks. Scarred by life's hardships, this champion won his final race in his category—the 1950 Palermo-Monte Pellegrino—before dying in his bed two years later, a fate he had always feared. Admittedly, due to space constraints, we couldn't include some deserving figures, including personal friends. We regret not being able to feature everyone, but such a task would have been impossible. Nevertheless, we are confident that this selection honors the vast and diverse world of racing drivers. Behind every name in this book lies a story—sometimes incredible and always meaningful. Of course, racing biographies offer more than just tales of speed. Take "Williams," born William Grover-Williams, for example. The first-ever winner of the Monaco Grand Prix in 1929, driving a Bugatti, he joined the French Resistance during World War II and tragically died in a German concentration camp. Alongside him, countless drivers—some famous, others obscure—have penned extraordinary chapters in history, often less tragic but no less fascinating. Our hope is that this book inspires readers to delve deeper into the world of motorsport, following the same passion that has driven nearly every racer, champion, or not—a passion that we, personally, have never lost.

Following pages: With seven world titles under his belt, Michael Schumacher is the most successful driver in Formula 1 history. He stood atop the podium ninety-one times.

POTENZA
BRIDGESTONE
BRIDGESTONE
Shell
vodafone
FIAT
1
BRIDGESTONE
Shell
vodafone
BRIDGESTONE

vodafone
FIAT
Schuberth
AMD

In this iconic picture, Tazio Nuvolari greets the crowd beside the Vanderbilt Cup, which he won in New York in October 1936.

TAZIO NUVOLARI

Myth, hero, legend . . . how often have these words been overused to describe drivers who were “merely” great champions and nothing more? In the history of motorsport, if there’s one true hero who passed into legend, it’s undoubtedly Tazio Nuvolari. And certainly, no driver has captured the imagination quite like the diminutive man from Castel d’Ario, a small town near Mantua once known as Casteldario, where a monument in the square commemorates its greatest champion. Nuvolari’s exploits were amplified by an era without television, turning him into a larger-than-life figure. A favorite son of a regime eager to glorify its heroes, Nuvolari’s incredible achievements and what Enzo Ferrari once described as “inhuman” courage remain unmatched. The crowning jewel in his long string of victories came at the 1935 German Grand Prix at the Nürburgring. Nuvolari, who referred to curves as his “resources,” had to navigate over 160 of them on the nearly 14-mile (23-kilometer) track—one of the most challenging circuits in the world. And he did so behind the wheel of a 330-horsepower Alfa Romeo P3, taking on the mighty Mercedes and Auto Union teams, whose cars boasted 460 and 375 horsepower, respectively. Under Adolf Hitler’s gaze, the Germans hadn’t even considered the possibility of losing. Yet, Nuvolari applied relentless pressure, and in the final lap, Manfred von Brauchitsch, the “Baron of Mercedes,” damaged his tires while trying to hold off the Italian. Astonishingly, Nuvolari had brought his own Italian national anthem record to play during the podium ceremony, confident he wouldn’t be defeated—even in the lion’s den. From that day on, the Germans dubbed him “Der Teufel” (the Devil), while in Italy, he was affectionately called “Nivola” or “the Flying Mantuan.”

Loved by fans, Nuvolari was involved in a fierce rivalry with fellow Italian driver Achille Varzi. Their duels predated even the famed Coppi-Bartali cycling battles, igniting debates in Italian squares and bars. A legendary victory at the 1930 Mille Miglia involved a daring maneuver in the dark, where Nuvolari allegedly turned off his headlights to overtake Varzi’s identical Alfa Romeo and steal the win. Born into a wealthy farming family, Nuvolari began his racing career on motorcycles. Neither the many crashes nor injuries could deter him; he even won a rain-soaked race in 1925 (the Nations motorcycle Grand Prix) with bandages covering his injuries. After a serious motorcycle accident in 1929, he triumphed in the Coppa Ciano with a plaster corset holding his torso together. His years at Alfa Romeo, under the sporting direction of Enzo Ferrari, brought numerous victories, including iconic races like the Tourist Trophy, the Targa Florio, and the 24 Hours of Le Mans, as well as Grand Prix events in Monaco, France,

28

and Italy. Only the overwhelming dominance of German cars prevented him from achieving more that he truly deserved.

Privately, Nuvolari was far from fortunate, despite his wealth and fame. The deaths of his two sons, Alberto in 1937 and Giorgio later, cast a shadow over his life. It's said that he then feared only one thing: dying in his bed. In 1938, at the age of forty-six, Nuvolari was called upon by Auto Union to replace Bernd Rosemeyer, who had tragically died attempting a speed record. Driving a powerful and notoriously challenging single-seater car, the Mantuan astonished everyone by winning the Italian and British Grand Prix.

Left: Monte Carlo, 1933. The Alfa Romeo of the Mantuan champion passes the Bugatti of Achille Varzi, his greatest rival throughout his career.

Above: Nuvolari urges his mechanics during a pit stop in the 1935 German Grand Prix, where he achieved one of his greatest victories.

TAZIO NUVOLARI *CASTEL D'ARIO 11-16-1892; MANTUA 8-11-1953*

MAJOR WINS: *GROME GP, GARDA CIRCUIT (1927); TRIPOLI GP, ALESSANDRIA CIRCUIT (1928); MILLE MIGLIA, TOURIST TROPHY (1930); TARGA FLORIO, COPPA CIANO (1931); MONACO GP, TARGA FLORIO, ITALIAN GP, FRENCH GP, COPPA CIANO, COPPA ACERBO (1932); TUNIS GP, MILLE MIGLIA, EIFELRENNEN, NÎMES GP, 24 HOURS OF LE MANS, BELGIAN GP, COPPA CIANO, NICE GP, TOURIST TROPHY (1933); GP PAU, GERMAN GP, COPPA CIANO, NICE GP (1935); PENYA RHIN GP, HUNGARIAN GP, MILAN CIRCUIT, COPPA CIANO, MODENA CIRCUIT, VANDERBILT CUP (1936); MILAN CIRCUIT (1937); ITALIAN GP, DONINGTON GP (1938); YUGOSLAV GP (1939); ALBI GP (1946).*

In 1939, he claimed victory once again in Belgrade, in the last international race before the outbreak of World War II. After racing for many years and inhaling copious amounts of exhaust fumes, Nuvolari's lungs deteriorated. Yet, he continued racing after the war, winning in Albi in 1946 with a Maserati, only to faint after crossing the finish line. In 1947, while driving a Cisitalia, he was set to win another Mille Miglia, only to be stopped by an electrical failure. His retirement from the Mille Miglia the following year, after dominating the race behind the wheel of the Ferrari 166 in what would be his final display of brilliance, was deeply moving. A suspension failure deprived the fifty-five-year-old of a remarkable victory, having thrilled the crowd with a breathtaking performance that left all his rivals in awe. In the end, it was illness that defeated him, taking him away on August 11, 1953, just shy of his sixty-first birthday.

Above: After Bernd Rosemeyer's passing, Nuvolari joined Auto Union in 1938. With their car, he won at Donington, Monza, and Belgrade in 1939.

Right: The start of the 1933 Belgian Grand Prix. Nuvolari began in last place with his Maserati but ended up winning ahead of Achille Varzi's Bugatti.

BERND ROSEMEYER

It took only three years of international racing for Bernd Rosemeyer to be recognized as one of the greatest drivers of all time. Remembered as Tazio Nuvolari's strongest rival, the German champion delivered unforgettable performances behind the wheel of the temperamental and challenging Auto Union car. His name is inseparably linked with the brand that hired him after testing him, along with other drivers, during the winter of 1934–1935 at the Nürburgring. Before then, Bernd had only raced motorcycles, yet he quickly matched the times of Hans Stuck, the team's most experienced driver. The Auto Union Grand Prix car, designed by the brilliant Ferdinand Porsche, was revolutionary in many ways. It featured a mid-mounted 16-cylinder engine, independent suspension, and an aerodynamic body. Its 5-liter engine delivered 375 horsepower, making it exceptionally difficult to control at high speeds due to narrow tires, immense power, and an unusual weight distribution.

Courage and honesty were Rosemeyer's hallmarks. Born in 1909 in Lingen, Lower Saxony, he swiftly climbed to the top of motorsport without fear of a challenge that might have intimidated others. By his second race at the Nürburgring, he was already fighting for the lead with Rudolf Caracciola's Mercedes, forging a rivalry and friendship that lasted until the end. Rosemeyer, for his part, was so likable that he won over everyone, including his rivals. His bold driving style at the Nürburgring, characterized by spectacular, controlled drifts with the rear of the car, earned him a permanent spot as a lead driver alongside Stuck and Varzi. At the Coppa Acerbo in Pescara, after dueling with Nuvolari, a pit stop for tire changes set him back. Determined to recover, Rosemeyer braked too hard, veered off the track, and reentered at full speed, threading the car between a bridge and a telegraph pole. He finished second behind Varzi. Ferdinand Porsche measured the gap he passed through—it was only 1.5 inches (4 centimeters) wider than the car itself! Rosemeyer claimed his first victory at the Czechoslovakian Grand Prix, his ninth race in a car.

Around this time, he met Elly Beinhorn, a celebrated German aviator far more famous than he was. Just months later, on July 13, 1936, Bernd and Elly married, choosing the date because it was their shared lucky number. Inspired by her passion, Rosemeyer began flying planes alongside her. The year 1936 marked the peak of Rosemeyer's career. Auto Union upgraded their engine from 5 to 6 liters, boosting power from 375 to 520 horsepower. Rosemeyer dominated the European Championship, which consisted of four Grand Prix races, winning three of them and excelling in both circuit and hill climb events. His Nürburgring performance under a thick fog left spectators astounded; his lap times in the final stages seemed superhuman, fueling myths about his extraordinary reflexes and vision. In 1937, Mercedes introduced the near-unbeatable W125, yet the Auto Union champion still managed to win the Eifelrennen at the

Rosemeyer celebrates his Vanderbilt Cup victory in 1937, one of his final triumphs with Auto Union.

BERND ROSEMEYER — *LINGEN 10-14-1909*
MÖRFELDEN-WALLDORF 01-28-1938

MAJOR WINS: *CZECHOSLOVAKIAN GP (1935); EIFELRENNEN, GERMAN GP, COPPA ACERBO, SWISS GP, ITALIAN GP (1936); VANDERBILT CUP, EIFELRENNEN, COPPA ACERBO, DONINGTON GP (1937).*

Left: Ferdinand Porsche assists Rosemeyer in the record-breaking car with which he set speed records in October 1937

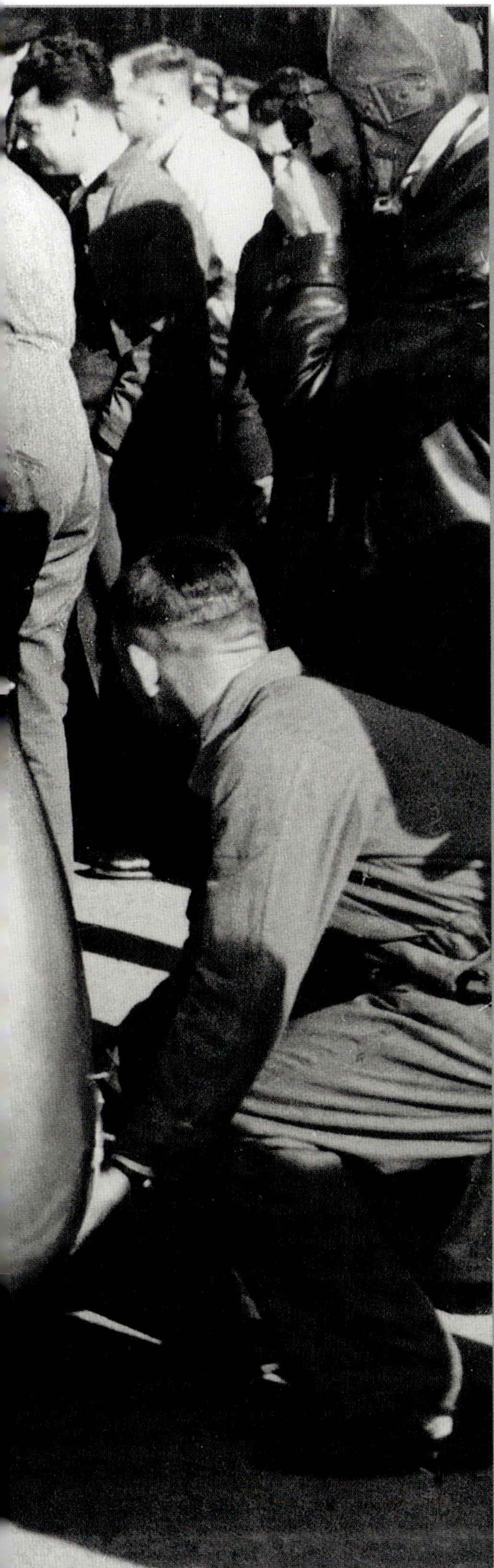

Nürburgring, the Coppa Acerbo in Pescara, and the Vanderbilt Cup in the United States. In October, Bernd set several speed records on the Autobahn between Frankfurt and Darmstadt, in a showdown that pitted Auto Union against Mercedes—and, naturally, him against Caracciola. After losing to Mercedes in October, the Stuttgart manufacturer modified its car for another attempt on January 28, 1938, the day Caracciola achieved a new land speed record with a peak of 268.9 mph (432.7 km/h). Just an hour and a half later, Auto Union rolled out its revised car, not designed by Porsche but by Robert Eberan von Eberhorst's team. Conditions were windy, and Caracciola considered warning his friend against attempting the run, but as a competitor himself, he refrained from interfering with his rival. On Rosemeyer's second run, while traveling at over 273.4 mph (440 km/h), a gust of wind caused the car to lose control near the Mörfelden-Walldorf exit. It disintegrated over 1,968.5 feet (600 meters), and Rosemeyer's body was found at the edge of a forest. A memorial now stands at the site. Caracciola once said of him, "Bernd does not know fear, and sometimes, that's not a good thing." His tragic death left behind a widow and a newborn son, Bernd Jr., only two and a half months old.

Above: Rosemeyer, cigarette in hand, photographed alongside Ernst von Delius and Nino Farina at the Roosevelt Raceway during the Vanderbilt Cup.

NINO FARINA

The first Formula 1 World Champion was practically born behind the wheel. Giuseppe Farina, known to all as Nino, came from a wealthy Turin family and had already learned to drive before turning ten. This might not seem surprising, as in the early 1910s, driver's licenses were yet to exist, and cars were a luxury few could afford. Nino was the son of Giovanni, a metalworking entrepreneur and brother of the famous "Pinin," who would go on to establish the Pininfarina design company.

Before starting his racing career, Nino Farina earned a law degree and trained to become a lawyer. Simultaneously, during his military service, he distinguished himself as a skilled cavalry officer. His passion for racing eventually prevailed, although he had to wait until he was twenty-five to debut at the Aosta-Grand Saint Bernard hill climb in 1932. Recklessly ambitious, he ran off the road attempting to beat his father, who was driving a similar Alfa Romeo, breaking his collarbone and sustaining various injuries. This marked the start of a career peppered with crashes, despite a driving style widely praised for its precision and control. Unlike his peers, he drove with straight arms and moved the wheel only as much as was strictly necessary, while others appeared to wrestle with their cars. In life, Farina could be abrasive, and as a driver, he was a relentless competitor, hard to overtake or defend against. By 1934, Farina had joined the top racing circuit and gained the admiration of Tazio Nuvolari. In 1936, he joined Scuderia Ferrari, which at the time, as is well known, competed with Alfa Romeo cars. His reputation as a tough driver grew with each race, unfortunately bolstered by two incidents that resulted in the deaths of rival drivers. In 1937, he won at Posillipo during a period dominated by German single-seaters, accumulating victories that secured him the Italian championship title through 1939. In 1940, he claimed victory at the Tripoli Grand Prix with an Alfa Romeo 158, just before the war robbed him of the prime years of his career.

After the war, Farina returned to the driver's seat despite being over forty and married to Elsa Giaretto, a member of Turin's elite society. Following strong performances and notable wins with Alfa Romeo and Maserati in Europe and South America, Farina was recruited by Alfa Romeo to compete in the inaugural Formula 1 World Championship. After racing

The first World Champion in Formula 1 history won at Silverstone, Bern, and Monza in 1950 before claiming the championship title with Alfa Romeo.

NINO FARINA	*TURIN 10-30-1906* *AIGUEBELLE 06-30-1966*
GP ENTERED	*33*
F1 WINS	*5*
POLE POSITIONS	*5*
F1 WORLD CHAMPIONSHIPS	*1950*

The finish of the first Grand Prix in history, the British Grand Prix at Silverstone in 1950. It was won by the driver from Turin in the Alfa Romeo 158.

alongside Nuvolari and teaming up with Luigi Fagioli and a certain Juan Manuel Fangio, Farina achieved three victories—at Silverstone, Bern, and, most memorably, Monza—ultimately outpacing Fangio, considered the greatest driver of the era. Later, however, he had to accept Fangio's dominance, as the Argentinian claimed the first of his five titles with Alfa Romeo. After Alfa Romeo's withdrawal, Farina joined Ferrari, which in 1952 and 1953 boasted the championship-winning 500 F2 car, designed for the new regulations. Unfortunately, his path to the title was blocked by another champion: Alberto Ascari. In 1952, Farina pushed hard to compete with his younger teammate, enduring multiple crashes but still managing to finish second in the championship. The following year started poorly, with an off-track excursion at the Argentine Grand Prix to avoid a young spectator who had wandered onto the circuit. Farina's Ferrari ended up in the crowd, killing ten spectators and injuring

Behind the wheel, Farina's style was composed and elegant. He kept his arms straight and moved the wheel only as much as necessary.

twenty-six, according to official reports. The season improved with Ascari's retirement at the Nürburgring, giving Farina his last Formula 1 victory. At nearly forty-seven years old, he remains the oldest driver to win a Grand Prix from start to finish. In 1954, Farina stayed with Ferrari but suffered more accidents, including a serious crash at Monza during a sports car race in the Ferrari Mondial, which left him with severe burns on his legs. By 1955, he needed powerful painkillers to compete, yet he still fought like a lion, finishing third at the Belgian Grand Prix. At the end of the season, he retired, though he briefly returned to attempt the Indianapolis 500 in 1956 and 1957, without success. He eventually became an Alfa Romeo and Jaguar dealer. However, Farina's driving habits on the road mirrored his track style. In 1966, while en route to the French Grand Prix in Reims, his Lotus Cortina crashed into a telegraph pole in Aiguebelle. Approaching sixty, Nino Farina died instantly.

JUAN MANUEL FANGIO

At first glance, Juan Manuel Fangio didn't even look like a race car driver, yet he is unanimously regarded as one of the greatest of all time, securing five World Championships in just seven active Formula 1 seasons. In total, he participated in only fifty-one Grand Prix races but won twenty-four of them, driving for Alfa Romeo, Mercedes, Ferrari, and Maserati. Fangio debuted in Formula 1 at the age of thirty-nine. He was short, slightly balding, and had a bit of a belly. He also had bowed legs, earning him the nickname "El Chueco" (the Bowlegged One) from his childhood days playing soccer with friends. In 1950, he won his second Formula 1 race in Monte Carlo, though the championship title slipped away in the final race to Nino Farina. It could be seen as a mere bump in the road because, from that point on, apart from Ascari and Ferrari's dominance in 1952 and 1953, Fangio became virtually unbeatable until his retirement. Younger drivers called him "Maestro" in recognition of his unmatched skill and poise. During an era when death lurked around every corner, Fangio had an extraordinary ability to calculate and control the inevitable risks. This might explain why he never won the Mille Miglia—a grueling race requiring constant improvisation and reckless risk-taking across 1,000 miles (approx. 1,600 kilometers) of treacherous terrain, including high-speed straights, mountain passes, and city streets.

Fangio was born in Balcarce, Argentina, to a family of Italian immigrants from Abruzzo who had settled south of Buenos Aires. Fascinated by cars from a young age, he began working as a mechanic almost immediately after finishing school. By the age of twelve, he was already driving cars in and out of the shop, learning the basics of handling treacherous, often-unpaved roads. He entered his first races at twenty-five, driving a Ford Model A that had previously served as a taxi. After acquiring a Chevrolet, Fangio achieved success in road races, gaining fame in Argentina before World War II. In 1948, with financial backing from the Argentine government under Juan Perón, he came to Europe with Oscar Gálvez, competing in Maserati cars and impressing enough to secure a contract with Alfa Romeo in 1950. Before his Formula 1 debut, however, he endured a harrowing experience during a road race in Argentina, where an accident claimed the life of his co-driver and friend, Daniel Urrutia. Despite his naturally reserved demeanor, Fangio was deeply sensitive and became one of the first drivers to hire a manager, the Italian Marcello Giambertone. He always measured his words, speaking in his distinct metallic tone, and preferred to have Giambertone handle negotiations with car manufacturers—a practice that greatly annoyed Enzo Ferrari in 1956 when the now-renowned Argentine

Juan Manuel Fangio is considered one of the greatest drivers of all time, not just for his five world titles but for his twenty-four victories in fifty-one races.

JUAN MANUEL FANGIO — *BALCARCE 06-24-1911* / *BUENOS AIRES 07-17-1995*

GP ENTERED	*51*
F1 WINS	*24*
POLE POSITIONS	*29*
F1 WORLD CHAMPIONSHIPS	*1951, 1954, 1955, 1956, 1957*

MERCEDES 2
VIGZOL
START

champion joined his team. He would arrive at races accompanied by his partner, Andreina Berruet, known as "Beba," whom he could never marry because she was already wed.

Fangio's first world title came in 1951, even as Ferrari grew increasingly competitive with wins from González and Ascari. In 1952, a serious non-championship crash at Monza nearly ended his career. After driving overnight from Ireland to Italy following a BRM race, he crashed his Maserati at the Lesmo curve, suffering spinal injuries that sidelined him for the season. In 1953, with Ferrari dominating Formula 1, Fangio still managed to win the Italian Grand Prix with Maserati.

The next two years were triumphant at Mercedes, despite the fierce competition from his fast and aggressive teammate Stirling Moss. Fangio joined Ferrari in 1956, winning another championship, and returned to Maserati in 1957, taking on Ferrari's top British drivers, Hawthorn and Collins.

By this point, some believed the forty-six-year-old champion was past his prime, but Fangio's skill and class proved otherwise. He reclaimed the championship with victories in Argentina, Monaco, France, and Germany. At the Nürburgring, Fangio staged one of his most legendary comebacks, recovering a fifty-second deficit to Mike Hawthorn and Peter Collins to win by eight seconds after smashing the lap record in qualifying. Fangio returned to racing in 1958, perhaps reluctantly, but retired after the tragic death of Luigi Musso at the French Grand Prix. After moving to Argentina, he focused on his business ventures, including managing a Mercedes dealership in Balcarce. He passed away in 1995 from kidney disease.

Left: Fangio dominated two consecutive World Championships with the Mercedes W196, which sometimes featured aerodynamic wheel covers. *Above*: Fangio (*left*, No. 2) starts from the front row of the 1955 Monaco Grand Prix alongside Ascari in a Lancia and Moss in a Mercedes. The Argentinian retired from that race.

ALBERTO ASCARI

The story of Alberto Ascari, and especially his untimely end, is steeped in almost unbelievable superstitions. The Milanese driver, World Champion in 1952 and 1953 with Ferrari, detested numbers like 13 and 17. He would even stop his car on the road if a black cat crossed it, waiting for someone else to pass first. He always wore the same racing gear and his signature blue helmet, refusing to let anyone else touch them. These superstitions were partly influenced by the death of his father, Antonio Ascari, also a racing driver, who died in an accident at Montlhéry on July 26, 1925—a date that is a multiple of the dreaded number 13.

Irresistibly drawn to engines, Alberto first fell in love with motorcycles, debuting in a regular race at just eighteen years old in 1936. He soon switched to speed trials and joined the official Bianchi team. His debut in car racing came during the shortened 1940 Mille Miglia, driving the first-ever Ferrari, the Auto Avio Costruzioni, which Ascari purchased with earnings from his vehicle dealership. His friendship with Luigi and Emilio Villoresi led him to meet Mietta, whom he married in 1942 during the war, and with whom he had two children, Antonio (known as "Tonino") and Patrizia. Alberto returned to racing in 1947 with a Cisitalia before being recruited by Maserati. After a crash in Argentina in January 1949, he decided to switch to Ferrari alongside Gigi Villoresi, beginning a partnership that brought him great success. Victories came quickly, both in Formula 2 and in sports car events, culminating in a win at the Italian Grand Prix at Monza, which cemented his reputation as one of the world's best drivers. Before his dominant seasons in 1952 and 1953, Ascari won the German and Italian Grands Prix in 1951. Like Fangio, who reportedly feared no other rival but him, Ascari did not have an athletic build despite maintaining a healthy diet and staying moderately active. As he rose to fame, he was given the nickname "Ciccio" ("Chubby") due to his stocky frame. Although he disliked it, the name became quite popular among fans. He owned a house on Corso Sempione in Milan and spent winters at his second home in Santa Margherita Ligure. He enjoyed skiing and skeet shooting, frequently visiting Cervinia and Cortina. A devoted and loving father, Ascari confided in close friends his fear that his children might grow too attached to him, given the very real possibility of a fatal accident in his line of work.

Ascari's dominance came with the regulation changes that made the Ferrari 500 F2 an unbeatable car in 1952 and 1953. Aside from the Indianapolis 500, which he entered but did not finish, Ascari won every championship race in 1952 and followed up with five wins out of eight in 1953. In 1954, he signed with Lancia to drive the stunning D50, though the car's development lagged. He occasionally raced with Maserati, securing a consola-

Alberto Ascari with the Lancia D50 during the 1955 Valentino Grand Prix, a non-championship race he won

ALBERTO ASCARI — *MILAN 07-13-1918* / *MONZA 05-25-1955*

GP ENTERED	*32*
F1 WINS	*13*
POLE POSITIONS	*14*
F1 WORLD CHAMPIONSHIPS	*1952, 1953*

tion victory at the Mille Miglia, and returned to Ferrari at Monza, where he led most of the race before losing the win just seven laps from the end. Ascari's Formula 1 debut with Lancia at the season's end brought pole position but also a retirement. By 1955, Ascari seemed to fear the year itself, as he had reached the age his father was when he died. After two non-championship wins, the Milanese driver led the Monaco Grand Prix but ended up in the harbor after a front-wheel lockup at the chicane. Coincidentally, his car bore the number 26. He escaped with minor bruises and a broken nose. Four days later, he received a call from Eugenio Castellotti, inviting him to Monza for testing ahead of the Trofeo Supercortemaggiore. Strangely, Ascari agreed, and during a midday break, he took Castellotti's Ferrari 750 Monza for a test lap wearing a shirt and Castellotti's helmet. No one could ever explain why Ascari chose to do something his superstitions would have absolutely forbidden—perhaps it was because he had surpassed, by two days, the age at which his father had met his fatal end: He was exactly 36 years, 10 months, and 13 days old, while Antonio Ascari had died at 36 years, 10 months, and 11 days old. On May 26, 1955 (yet another multiple of 13!), on his third test lap, as he began to push harder, Ascari fatally crashed at the Vialone curve, now named after him. The cause of the crash remains a mystery, with theories ranging from a differential or tire failure to a worker crossing the track.

Above: The start of the 1953 Monza race, where Fangio's Maserati (winner) lines up between Farina and teammate Ascari, who was racing his final Grand Prix with Ferrari

Above: Alberto Ascari celebrates victory with Ferrari at the 1951 Italian Grand Prix, his second win and a prelude to his later triumphs.

STIRLING MOSS

By nearly unanimous agreement—not just among the British—Stirling Moss is considered the greatest driver never to win a Formula 1 World Championship. Born in London in 1929, Moss grew up in a stately home with an attached park, where he began driving at the tender age of six in an Austin 7. That same car is still proudly kept at his London home in Mayfair, which had been his operational base for decades. His father, Alfred, was a dentist who had been involved in racing, and even his mother had taken part in regularity and rally events. However, Stirling and his sister, Pat, earned their first money in equestrian competitions. While Pat, who later married rally champion Erik Carlsson, continued with horses, Stirling—encouraged by his family—began racing cars. His first purchase was a Cooper 500, which he used to debut in hill climbs and circuit racing. By the age of twenty-one, he was already regarded as a fearless young talent, winning the Tourist Trophy at Dundrod in a private Jaguar XK120, which earned him a spot on the official team. Around this time, HWM recruited him for Formula 1, where he stood out despite frequent retirements caused by an unreliable car.

In 1951, Moss was supposed to race for Ferrari, but upon arriving in Bari, he was bitterly disappointed to find his car had been reassigned to Piero Taruffi. Vowing never to forget the slight, he swore he would race and win only in British cars for the rest of his career. His best result that year came in the Monte Carlo Rally, where he finished second in a Sunbeam, showcasing his versatility. Realizing that British cars wouldn't allow him to compete at the highest level, Moss purchased a Maserati 250F with his father's help and returned to the Formula 1 circuits, flying past the competition. Although frequent retirements plagued him, Mercedes took notice and signed him as teammate to the legendary Juan Manuel Fangio in 1955. That season, dominated by Fangio's expertise, Moss finally claimed his first Grand Prix victory at Aintree. Not long before, the British champion compared the Mille Miglia to entering the Monte Carlo tunnel, where for a couple of seconds drivers felt as though they were leaping into the void—except that, in the case of the Italian road race, that sensation lasted for 1,000 miles (1,600 km). In 1955, Moss won the Mille Miglia with Mercedes at a record average speed of over 97.5 mph (157 km/h), accompanied by journalist Denis Jenkinson, who developed a kind of roadbook to help Moss adjust his pace for the race's various challenges. Moss and Fangio also seemed poised to win the 24 Hours of Le Mans that year, but Mercedes withdrew all their cars at 4 a.m. following the catastrophic accident involving Pierre Levegh's car, which killed over eighty spectators. At the end of the year, the German manufacturer withdrew from racing, forcing Moss to return to Maserati, this time as an official

A young Stirling Moss celebrates his victory in the first Aintree 200 in 1955, driving his Maserati 250F.

STIRLING MOSS — *WEST KENSINGTON 09-17-1929* — *LONDON 04-12-2020*

GP ENTERED	*66*
F1 WINS	*16*
POLE POSITIONS	*16*

team member. In 1956, he won the Monaco and Italian Grand Prix, but the title once again went to Fangio. By then a darling of the British press, Moss embraced the classic "bon vivant" lifestyle of drivers of the era. While he avoided heavy drinking, he had numerous romantic escapades before marrying Canadian Katie Molson—of the renowned brewing family—in 1957. The marriage didn't last, but Moss eventually found lasting happiness with his third wife, Susie, whom he married in 1980. In 1957, Moss joined Vanwall and narrowly lost the 1958 title to Mike Hawthorn and his Ferrari by a single point. Ironically, Moss had helped Hawthorn avoid disqualification in the decisive Moroccan Grand Prix. It was the fourth time Moss finished second in the World Championship standings. The string of Grand Prix victories didn't end there. Even driving Rob Walker's Lotus—he joined the privateer team after Vanwall's withdrawal—Moss managed to outperform the competition on more than one occasion. The victory at Monte Carlo in 1961 with the Lotus 18 is fondly remembered by his fans, but the Englishman also claimed first place at the Nürburgring, the most challenging circuit on the calendar. In 1962, after Rob Walker and Moss had reached an agreement with Ferrari to race a Maranello single-seater in the team's colors, fate took a definitive turn. On Easter Sunday at Goodwood, Moss crashed his Lotus into an embankment. It took thirty minutes to extract him from the wreckage, unconscious. Moss woke from his coma thirty-five days later, but the injuries he sustained ended his racing career. Knighted in 2000, Sir Stirling Moss remains one of the most iconic figures in motorsport history.

Left: Moss looks pensive in the pits at Monza during the 1954 Italian Grand Prix, where he raced his Maserati 250F.

Above: The start of the 1955 British Grand Prix at Aintree. Moss jumped ahead of Fangio to win the race, finishing ahead of his teammate.

ALFONSO DE PORTAGO

More than for his racing career or victories, Alfonso de Portago is remembered for the fairy-tale life he led during his short time on Earth. An heir to Spanish nobility, he was the son of a nobleman and the grandson of King Alfonso XIII. According to his astonishingly elaborate business card, his full name was Alfonso Antonio Vicente Eduardo Ángel Blas Francisco de Borja Cabeza de Vaca y Leighton, Carvajal y Aire, XVII Marquis de Portago, XII Count of Mejorada. His equally aristocratic father died young in a polo match, and Alfonso, the son of Olga Leighton, a beautiful Irishwoman, faced few obstacles in pursuing his passions. He spent much of his childhood and adolescence in Biarritz, where he quickly learned not only Spanish and English but also French and Italian. With vast wealth at his disposal, he developed a love for airplanes at an early age. At just seventeen, he lost his pilot's license—earned in the United States—after flying under a railroad bridge in Palm Beach, California, to win a $500 bet. Though he lost his license, he won the wager, embodying his daredevil nature. De Portago excelled in a variety of sports, starting with equestrianism and polo before moving on to swimming and diving, where he even became the Spanish national champion.

By age twenty, he was married to American model Carroll McDaniel and became the father of two children. However, married life didn't suit him, as he preferred to travel the world carefree. Though he never divorced, he had many other relationships, aided by his tall, athletic build, black hair, light eyes, and innate charm. De Portago was the quintessential wealthy and attractive 1950s playboy who women found irresistible. He traveled light, often without luggage, but always carried a roll of cash to procure whatever he needed. De Portago's introduction to racing came through Edmund Nelson, a regular at the Plaza Hotel in New York, which was Alfonso's usual residence in the city. It was there that he met Luigi Chinetti, the US importer of Ferraris, who took him along as a co-driver in the 1953 Carrera Panamericana. De Portago soon bought a Ferrari 250 Mille Miglia and learned the basics of racing from Harry Schell, an American driver living in Paris. In the racing world, perhaps to acknowledge his noble lineage, people mistakenly referred to him by his title, Marquis. To close friends and fellow adventurers, he was simply "Fon." With Schell, he achieved his first significant results in sports car races from Buenos Aires to Sebring.

By 1955, de Portago was driving a Ferrari Formula 1 car he had purchased himself but broke his leg in a crash at Silverstone. Undeterred, he returned to racing later that season. During the winter, he formed a Spanish bobsled team for the 1956 Cortina d'Ampezzo Olympics. Competing in the two-man bobsled event with no prior reputation in the sport, he managed to finish fourth, just shy of a medal. In 1956, de Portago was signed by Ferrari's official team alongside stars like Fangio, Collins, Musso, and Castellotti. Initially intended only for sports car races, he also found himself in Formula 1, earning a second-place finish at the British Grand Prix at Silverstone, sharing the car with Collins. At the end of the year, he won the Tour de France in a Ferrari 250 GT with his loyal co-driver Nelson. By then, "Fon" was an internationally recognized driver and entered the 1957 season with high hopes. Ever the risk taker, after his 1955 crash he had declared that he would become Formula 1 World Champion before turning thirty-five. In the year's first Grand Prix, he finished fifth with Ferrari and later secured third place at the 1000 km Buenos Aires alongside Peter Collins. After his relationship with model Dorian Leigh, de Portago captured the heart of Linda Christian, the American actress recently separated from Tyrone Power. May brought the Mille Miglia, the dangerous Italian road race that de Portago hadn't wanted to enter. Ferrari initially assigned him a 250 GT but later replaced it with the 335S, a sports prototype, to stand in for Musso. Teamed with his faithful co-driver Nelson, he reached Rome by 11 a.m. for a pit stop, where Linda Christian greeted him with a passionate kiss, immortalized in photos of the time. De Portago and Nelson were fifth at the Bologna stop, three-quarters into the race. The left front tire was wearing abnormally due to contact with the fender. When asked if they wanted to replace it, de Portago refused, fearing he would lose time and his position to Gendebien, who was driving the 250 GT initially assigned to him. At Guidizzolo, just 31 miles (50 km) from the finish line, de Portago and Nelson's tragic fate unfolded. Presumably due to a tire blowout, their Ferrari swerved on a straightaway at about 155 mph (250 km/h), struck a telegraph pole, and crashed into a group of spectators, killing nine, including five children. Both "Fon" and Nelson died instantly in a horrific accident that marked the end of the Mille Miglia, deemed too dangerous to continue.

Alfonso de Portago, heir to Spanish nobility, was a colorful and unforgettable figure in motorsport history and a true all-around athlete.

ALFONSO DE PORTAGO *LONDON 10-11-1928*
GUIDIZZOLO 05-12-1957

GP ENTERED *5*

MIKE HAWTHORN

The first British Formula 1 World Champion was a colorful character who often reminded people that "life is short." Mike Hawthorn's motto excused his natural inclination for (sometimes excessive) fun, which had followed him since adolescence. The son of a garage owner in Farnham, Surrey, Hawthorn quickly developed a passion for racing by accompanying his father, Leslie, to the Brooklands circuit. As a child, he spent much of his time at his father's Tourist Trophy Garage. Not an exceptional student, Mike received family support to debut in racing in 1950 at just twenty-one years old. Only two years later, in 1952, he was competing in his first single-seater—a Formula 2 Cooper-Bristol—with which he impressed by battling Gigi Villoresi's Ferrari in wet conditions. Villoresi recommended the young Englishman to Ferrari, and Hawthorn soon caught the attention of Jaguar's official team.

After less than two years of competition, Hawthorn debuted in Formula 1 at the 1952 Belgian Grand Prix in a Cooper-Bristol, finishing fourth. At the next race at Silverstone, he made it to the podium behind Ascari and Taruffi. By 1953, Hawthorn was part of Ferrari's official team alongside Ascari, Villoresi, and Farina. His meteoric rise reached a major milestone with a victory at the French Grand Prix in Reims, where the twenty-four-year-old defeated the great Juan Manuel Fangio in his Maserati.

Highs and lows followed. In 1954, a serious accident in Syracuse left Hawthorn burned, and the loss of his father in a road accident deeply affected him. That year, the dominance of German cars forced Hawthorn into a desperate chase in Formula 1, partially redeemed by a victory in the season's final Spanish Grand Prix.

Standing 6'2" tall, with blond hair and a booming voice, Mike Hawthorn was easily recognizable. On the track, he wore a helmet with a visor and always raced in his beloved bow tie or tie under his jacket. In Britain, a rivalry developed between Hawthorn and Stirling Moss, who could be considered one of the first true professionals in the sport, going so far as to abstain entirely from alcohol while still enjoying life off the track. Hawthorn, in contrast, loved indulgence, including heavy drinking, which likely cost him additional victories. By late 1954, Hawthorn returned to England to race in Formula 1 with Vanwall and in sports cars with Jaguar. However, serious health problems began to surface, with doctors diagnosing a kidney malformation requiring surgery to prevent infections and painful kidney stones. But the worst was yet to come. At Le Mans in 1955, while battling Fangio's Mercedes, Hawthorn suddenly

Mike Hawthorn in the cockpit of his Ferrari in the Monte Carlo pits, 1957. Beyond cars, he loved the high life and its excesses.

MIKE HAWTHORN — *MEXBOROUGH 04-10-1929* / *GUILDFORD 01-22-1959*

GP ENTERED	*43*
F1 WINS	*3*
POLE POSITIONS	*4*
F1 WORLD CHAMPIONSHIPS	*1958*

Winner Mike Hawthorn and runner-up Stirling Moss at the 1958 French Grand Prix in Reims, where Luigi Musso tragically lost his life

braked his Jaguar to enter the pits, triggering what became the deadliest accident in racing history. Pierre Levegh's car crashed into the crowd, killing over eighty spectators. Hawthorn's subsequent victory, shared with co-driver Ivor Bueb, sparked controversy as they celebrated on the podium despite the tragedy. The years 1955 and 1956 were particularly challenging for Hawthorn. Blamed by some for the Le Mans disaster, he struggled to achieve good results and suffered two harrowing crashes—at Goodwood in a BRM and at Oulton Park in a Lotus. Plagued by exhaustion and ongoing health problems, Hawthorn persisted despite his struggles, which weren't entirely caused by his penchant for the high life.

In 1957, he returned to Ferrari, joining Castellotti, Musso, and Peter Collins. He developed a deep friendship with Collins, often traveling with him and Collins's wife, Louise. Though he delivered some solid performances, the season was disappointing overall, with Fangio famously overtaking him at the Nürburgring.

The 1958 World Championship came at the end of a tragic season. Hawthorn's sole win came on the day Luigi Musso

The start of the **1957 Naples Grand Prix** at Posillipo, with Ferrari drivers Musso, Collins, and Hawthorn in the front row. They would be teammates again **during the tragic** 1958 season.

died while battling him for the lead at the French Grand Prix in Reims. That devastating season hit Hawthorn hardest with the loss of Collins, who crashed fatally at the Nürburgring in front of him. The championship-deciding race in Morocco saw Hawthorn needing only a second-place finish to claim the title over Stirling Moss, who had won three races to Hawthorn's one. Indeed, he finished second to Moss, securing the championship, but the race was marred by another severe accident. Stuart Lewis-Evans crashed and succumbed to his injuries six days later.

Hawthorn retired at twenty-nine, dedicating his championship to his father and planning to marry model Jean Howarth. Unbeknown to him, his kidney condition would leave him with less than eighteen months to live. After spending Christmas bedridden, Hawthorn resumed his usual lifestyle. On January 22, 1959, while returning from a party, he veered off the road in his Jaguar, struck a truck, and crashed into a tree near Guildford. Like his father, Mike Hawthorn died instantly, ending a series of tragic events that marked one of the darkest periods in racing history.

EUGENIO CASTELLOTTI

Cars were always in Eugenio Castellotti's DNA. The son of a lawyer from Lodi who had built a fortune in agriculture and land, Castellotti grew up surrounded by automobiles. As a child, he played with model cars, and as soon as he was old enough, he began driving real ones, speeding freely across his family's estates. On his eighteenth birthday, he obtained his driver's license and was gifted a Ferrari 166 MM Spider, which he drove from Lodi to Milan and back at record speeds, taking advantage of the empty roads at night. Speed became his passion. At just nineteen, Castellotti lost his father in late 1949. Free from constraints, he soon gravitated toward the world of racing. He made his debut in 1951 with his 166 MM in the Giro di Sicilia, though he retired after several off-road excursions. He reappeared at the Mille Miglia, finishing sixth in his category. His first victories came in 1952 with another Ferrari, a 225 S he purchased for that season. A member of the Scuderia Guastalla, Castellotti began associating with renowned drivers like Alberto Ascari and Gigi Villoresi. At the Mille Miglia, he impressed the audience by running in second place overall before crashing out due to his aggressive style. However, he redeemed himself with a second-place finish in Monte Carlo and victories in Oporto and Senigallia, always with the 225 S.

Eugenio caught Lancia's attention and was signed by the Turin team in 1953, debuting in the Carrera Panamericana—a Mexican equivalent of the perilous Mille Miglia. Despite driving an older car than Fangio and Taruffi, he finished third. In 1954, now teammates with Alberto Ascari, whom Castellotti idolized like an older brother, he found success primarily in hill climbs while gaining experience in sports cars alongside Ascari and Fangio. In 1955, he doubled his commitments, driving the beautiful Lancia D50 in Formula 1 and Ferrari in sports car races. At the Mille Miglia, his attempt to beat Moss and Jenkinson's record-breaking Mercedes ended with shredded tires and retirement. In Monte Carlo, Ascari famously plunged into the harbor with his Lancia while Castellotti finished second. Four days later, at Monza, he lent his Ferrari to Ascari, who wanted to test it during a midday break. Unable to refuse, Eugenio watched helplessly as his mentor fatally crashed. The loss devastated Castellotti, who was wracked with guilt over lending the car. Lancia subsequently withdrew from racing, and Eugenio competed in the Belgian Grand Prix as a private entrant, holding his own against Fangio and Moss's Mercedes. When Ferrari inherited Lancia's single-seaters, the Lodi-born driver transitioned to Ferrari's Formula 1 team.

By 1956, he felt ready for a breakthrough, but Ferrari's signing of Fangio and the emerging Musso dashed his hopes of becoming lead driver. Nonetheless, the Argentinian champion valued Castellotti as a teammate in endurance races, a compliment that deeply flattered him. Together, they won at Sebring, and Eugenio shone on his own at a rain-soaked Mille Miglia, where his Ferrari 290 MM dominated, securing massive gaps over the competition. The victory made him a household name across Italy. Known for his elegant style and charm, Castellotti also had numerous romantic entanglements. That summer, he fell for Delia Scala, a popular entertainer who had recently divorced. His mother, Angela, disapproved of the relationship, but Castellotti pursued Scala passionately, even proposing marriage, though she hesitated. Their relationship made headlines and became fodder for gossip in racing circles.

The 1957 season began with a retirement in the Argentine Grand Prix but improved with a sports car victory at the 1,000 km Buenos Aires, partnered with Perdisa. In early March, Delia Scala was performing in a play in Florence while Castellotti shuttled between Tuscany and Modena for Ferrari testing. On March 13, Maserati's Jean Behra broke the lap record at Modena, much to the chagrin of Enzo Ferrari, who placed great importance on that achievement and the rivalry with the Trident brand. The following day, determined to reclaim the record, Castellotti took to the track in a Lancia D50. Shortly after 5 p.m., his car crashed in the esses after the start/finish straight. Eugenio was thrown from the cockpit, sustaining injuries that proved fatal en route to the hospital. Speculation about the cause ranged from brake failure to personal turmoil over his relationship with Delia Scala, though no definitive explanation was ever found.

Castellotti with the Lancia he raced at the start of the 1955 season. Ascari's fatal crash led to Lancia's withdrawal, and Castellotti transitioned, along with the D50 cars, to Ferrari.

EUGENIO CASTELLOTTI *LODI 10-10-1930*
MODENA 03-14-1957

GP ENTERED	*14*
POLE POSITIONS	*1*

PETER COLLINS

Like Moss and Hawthorn, Peter Collins became a driver naturally, influenced by the environment in which he grew up. His father, Pat, was a car dealer in Worcestershire with a thriving business in Mustow Green, near Kidderminster. Peter was just fifteen when he convinced his father to join him in the Blackpool Rally, driving an Aston Martin. Born in 1931, young Collins earned his driver's license at only seventeen, and by the spring of 1949, he was on the track with a Cooper 500, facing fierce competitors like Stirling Moss. Gifted with undeniable natural talent, Collins amassed numerous victories in 1951, establishing himself as a promising driver. His skill behind the wheel often compensated for a lack of mechanical fine-tuning in his cars. During these years, he also learned to avoid excessive risks, having been shaken by the loss of two close friends in separate racing incidents. Off the track, Collins could have easily been mistaken for a movie star. Always polite and refined, he managed to convince Aston Martin and HWM to let him test their cars, and by 1952, he was racing for both teams. That year, he claimed a stunning victory in the 9 Hours of Goodwood in a DB3 Aston Martin alongside Pat Griffith. In HWM's Formula 2 cars, he found himself paired with Moss. To avoid mandatory military service and continue racing, Peter moved to Paris in 1953, a year when he won the demanding

Tourist Trophy, again with Aston Martin and Griffith. His career continued with Vanwall, which fielded him in 1954 with a Ferrari painted green, nicknamed the Thinwall Special. With 400 horsepower, it was a difficult car to handle, but Collins triumphed in the rain at Goodwood and Snetterton. In 1955, after racing with BRM as well, he was signed by Maserati for the Italian Grand Prix at Monza, though he retired. He also upset Aston Martin's management by agreeing to drive a Mercedes in the Targa Florio, winning alongside Stirling Moss.

On the advice of Mike Hawthorn, who had become a close friend, Ferrari signed Collins in 1956. On the team, he joined Musso, Castellotti, Gendebien, de Portago, and especially Fangio. Collins made history by giving up his car to Fangio during the decisive Italian Grand Prix at Monza. Although he had a remote chance at the title himself, Collins obeyed team orders and handed over his Ferrari to the Argentinian champion, a gesture that became legendary. Meanwhile, Collins secured his first Formula 1 victory at the Belgian Grand Prix, quickly followed by another win in France at Reims.

1957 was a pivotal year in Peter's life. In February, he married Louise Cordier, an American actress and the daughter of a UN assistant secretary. This ended his string of romantic escapades. With Fangio departing for Maserati, Ferrari brought back Mike Hawthorn. Collins and Hawthorn, close friends, affectionately called each other "mon ami mate," after characters in a British comic strip. They were so close that they reportedly decided to share their prize money, regardless of who finished higher. However, the season was underwhelming, with only a couple of wins at Syracuse and Posillipo. Notably, Fangio's epic comeback at the Nürburgring overshadowed Collins and Hawthorn, helping Fangio secure his fifth World Championship. Enzo Ferrari believed marriage had dulled Collins's edge, but he retained him for the 1958 season.

That tragic season left an indelible mark on motorsport history and Ferrari. Collins and his wife, Louise, moved to Monte Carlo, where they moored their new yacht. For travel, they often used Hawthorn's private plane, as the trio was nearly inseparable. Early victories with Phil Hill at Buenos Aires and Sebring in sports car races, along with a Formula 1 win at Silverstone in a non-championship race, hinted at a promising year. However, tragedy struck in July with the death of Musso at Reims. Collins and Hawthorn, however, appeared largely unaffected. At the British Grand Prix at Silverstone, Collins secured a decisive victory, leading nearly from start to finish. Fifteen days later, on the daunting Nürburgring circuit, the German Grand Prix took place. Perhaps the memory of Fangio's comeback still stung, but the fact remains that Collins was leading on the eleventh lap when Tony Brooks's Vanwall caught up and overtook him. He was trailing his compatriot when, at Pflanzgarten, he came in too wide and fast, right in front of Hawthorn, who was following closely. His Ferrari spun out, lifting off the ground. Thrown from the car, Collins struck his head against the only tree on the outside of the curve. He was rushed to a hospital in Bonn but succumbed to his injuries.

Peter Collins in the pits at Silverstone on the eve of the 1958 British Grand Prix, which he won with the Ferrari D246

PETER COLLINS *KIDDERMINSTER 11-06-1931*
BONN 08-03-1958

GP ENTERED *32*
F1 WINS *3*

LUIGI MUSSO

The story of Luigi Musso is intertwined, in many ways, with that of Eugenio Castellotti. Both were Italy's rising stars in the mid-1950s and shared several similarities, including wealthy family backgrounds. Like Castellotti, Musso lost his father early—at just sixteen years old in 1940. His father, Giuseppe Domenico, was a lawyer from Rome who amassed great wealth through government transport contracts in Shanghai and by founding a film production company in Italy. Luigi, the youngest of five siblings, was inspired to race by his older brothers, Luciano and Giuseppe. He also served briefly in the Air Force and married young in 1945. The marriage didn't last, and by 1950, Musso was already a father of two and had purchased his first race cars. In 1951, he was driving a Ferrari 166 MM. By the following year, he had switched to Maserati, placing eleventh at the Targa Florio. Maserati's official team began supporting him, leading to his victory in the Italian Sports Car Championship.

Musso had immense natural talent and drove with a composed, precise style that favored fast circuits, his preferred terrain. Always impeccably dressed, he had two major vices: a relentless smoking habit and an obsession with gambling. Like his brothers, Musso was drawn to cards and roulette, often wagering—and losing—significant sums. Among his lovers was Maria Teresa de Filippis, a trailblazing female driver renowned for her achievements in both Formula 1 and sports car racing. By 1954, Musso was an official Maserati driver, finishing second at the Mille Miglia and in the season-ending Spanish Grand Prix at Pedralbes. His most significant win came in the non-championship Pescara Grand Prix, which Musso dominated in a 250F. More successes followed in 1955, including victory at the Supercortemaggiore Grand Prix at Monza, the Italian Sports Car Championship, and third place in the Dutch Grand Prix. These achievements caught Enzo Ferrari's attention, and in 1956, Musso joined Ferrari, teaming up with Fangio, Collins, de Portago, Gendebien, and Castellotti. A fierce rivalry developed between Musso and Castellotti, who had hoped to become Ferrari's lead driver. Their battles culminated in the Italian Grand Prix at Monza, where both drivers retired after an intense duel for the lead. During that race, Musso refused to hand his car over to Fangio, angering Enzo Ferrari. Meanwhile, Castellotti claimed victory at the Mille Miglia, while Musso suffered an accident in a Ferrari 290 MM at the Nürburgring. The following winter, the two drivers reconciled during a brief vacation. Meanwhile, Musso had met a Florentine girl, Fiammetta Breschi, who was only eighteen when she fell in love with the Roman driver.

Eugenio Castellotti's death in early 1957 deeply affected Musso, who seemed visibly changed to those who knew him well. At the same time, his financial troubles mounted, stemming from his reckless gambling habits and poor investments, including an ill-fated American car dealership. In May, Musso narrowly avoided tragedy himself, as bronchitis kept him from driving the Ferrari that de Portago crashed in the Mille Miglia, killing several spectators. This incident further troubled Musso, though he rebounded with strong results, including a victory in the French Grand Prix at Reims—a non-championship race with a substantial prize that alleviated some of his financial woes.

Musso believed he could become World Champion with Ferrari and turned down an offer from BRM for the 1958 season. His campaign began promisingly, with second-place finishes in Argentina and Monaco, as well as wins in the Syracuse Grand Prix and the Targa Florio, the latter shared with Gendebien. A week after the 500 Miles of Monza, held on the high-speed oval and where he finished third alongside Phil Hill and Mike Hawthorn, the French Grand Prix at Reims was next on the calendar. Luigi saw the race as crucial and, on the eve of the event, received a telegram urging him to win to address his financial difficulties. Fangio had once confided in him that, with enough courage and skill, it was possible to take the first corner after the finish line without lifting off the throttle. On the tenth lap, in Hawthorn's slipstream and aiming to overtake him on the next straight, Musso decided to attempt it. However, that year's Ferrari was more powerful and approached the corner at higher speeds, so it could not maintain the trajectory, set by its driver at 161.5 mph (260 km/h). Luigi went off the track and was thrown from the car, dying almost instantly from internal injuries.

The yellow helmet was a hallmark of Luigi Musso's racing gear. The Roman driver lost his life at Reims in 1958 while battling teammate Hawthorn.

LUIGI MUSSO — *ROME 07-28-1924*
REIMS 07-06-1958

GP ENTERED 24
F1 WINS 1

JACK BRABHAM

In civilian clothes, Jack Brabham could hardly have been mistaken for one of the greatest drivers of all time. With his calm, family-man demeanor, it's easy to overlook the historic achievements of the three-time World Champion from Australia. Brabham made history as the only driver to win a Formula 1 title in a car he constructed himself. Born in 1926 near Sydney, he was the son of a grocer. Like many boys of his generation, he learned to drive at age twelve. By fifteen, he realized school wasn't for him and began working as a mechanic, studying in the evenings. After two years of service in the Royal Australian Air Force in 1946, he opened a repair shop and took an interest in midget car racing, encouraged by his American friend Johnny Schönberg, a competitor in the category. These cars, raced on dirt ovals, were basic single-seaters, and midget racing remains popular in the English-speaking world. Brabham built a car for Schönberg, and when his friend retired, he reluctantly began racing.

Victories came quickly, and Brabham soon moved on to circuit and hill climb racing. In the 1950s, he met fellow Australian Ron Tauranac, who shared his interest in car engineering. Together, they formed a partnership destined to become legendary. By the end of 1954, Brabham had amassed numerous wins in cars he either built or modified. Known for his reserved nature, he earned the nickname "Black Jack," both for his jet-black hair and his tenacious racing style. Riding a wave of success, Brabham decided to try his luck in Europe, intending to stay only one year before returning home

At the 1955 British Grand Prix at Silverstone, Brabham was on the grid in a Formula 1 Cooper, and despite being twenty-nine years old, his career took a dramatic turn. After an unsuccessful stint with a privately entered Maserati 250F, he returned to Cooper, whose cars, unlike other Formula 1 single-seaters, featured rear-mounted engines. Small and nimble, the Coopers dominated the late 1950s and the 1960s. Brabham made them famous by winning the World Championships in 1959 and 1960, with seven Grand Prix victories during his campaign. Married to Betty since 1951, Jack defied the stereotype of the flamboyant driver, even driving so cautiously on public roads that he frustrated his colleagues. However, he considered flying as an alternative for traveling across Europe and was among the first to purchase and pilot his own plane to get to races.

In 1962, Brabham and Tauranac founded Motor Racing Developments and took the bold step of becoming constructors. After initial retirements, they scored their first win at the 1964 French Grand Prix with Dan Gurney. A regulatory change

Jack Brabham won three World Championships and remains the only constructor-driver to achieve this feat in his own car.

JACK BRABHAM	HURSTVILLE 04-02-1926 GOLD COAST 05-19-2014
GP ENTERED	126
F1 WINS	14
POLE POSITIONS	13
F1 WORLD CHAMPIONSHIPS	1959, 1960, 1966

Left: The Australian champion driving the Brabham Repco at Silverstone in 1966

Right: Jack preparing for the 1964 Indianapolis 500 in his Brabham-Offenhauser. In a race that often eluded him, he was forced to retire.

in 1966, which introduced 3-liter engines, proved pivotal. The Australian-built Repco engines, derived from Oldsmobile designs, were a perfect match, and despite contemplating retirement, Brabham became the first driver to win a World Championship in a car bearing his name. With four victories, he claimed his third title, having already crossed the forty-year mark. Brabham's dominance continued into 1967, but it was his teammate, Denis Hulme, who won the World Championship. However, "Black Jack" still finished second overall, with two Grand Prix wins. In 1968, he recruited Jochen Rindt, followed by Jacky Ickx in 1969, but the results didn't match previous successes. Between seasons, he found joy in flying his Beechcraft from England to Australia.

In June 1969, a testing crash at Silverstone left him with a broken ankle, prompting thoughts of retirement, also to please his wife, Betty. However, the lack of a suitable replacement forced him to continue. Remarkably, at forty-four years old, Brabham won the South African Grand Prix, narrowly missed victory at Monaco due to an error in the final corner, and ran out of fuel at Brands Hatch while leading. Brabham remained competitive throughout 1970, the year of Jochen Rindt's posthumous championship, playing a leading role until the final Grand Prix in Mexico, where he retired while running third. Thus ended a career often underrated by the critics but marked by immense accomplishments from a man who, in the end, struggled to cross the street yet remained one of the best on the track. After selling his team to Bernie Ecclestone, Brabham enjoyed retirement on a farm in Australia. He was knighted in recognition of his achievements, the first postwar driver to receive the honor. Suffering from kidney disease, Jack Brabham passed away on May 19, 2014. His three sons, Geoff, Gary, and David, raced internationally but never matched their father's success.

52
ENCO

BRUCE McLAREN

Following the victories of Lauda, Prost, and Senna, McLaren is now a household name in Formula 1 and motorsport. Equally fascinating, however, is the story of its founder, which began in Auckland in 1937. Born into a family that owned a repair shop and service station, Bruce McLaren grew up surrounded by cars and engines. Life seemed promising, but it held a harsh surprise. At age nine, Bruce was diagnosed with Legg-Calvé-Perthes disease, initially mistaken for polio. This condition caused a lack of blood flow to the femur head, stunting bone development. McLaren spent two years in an orthopedic hospital, part of it in traction, before recovering. He overcame what could have been a devastating setback with courage and optimism, even organizing wheelchair races with his peers. The disease left his left leg slightly shorter, causing a limp and occasional hip pain.

Bruce's father, Les, was a passionate motorsport enthusiast, competing in hill climbs and time trials, and encouraged young Bruce to learn the basics of driving. Together, they prepared a vintage Austin 7 Ulster, which Bruce debuted in a hill climb at just fourteen years old. Two years later, he began competing regularly in increasingly powerful cars, shining in national championships. Besides driving, McLaren worked on his cars, studying ways to enhance their performance. His talent earned him a spot as the first driver selected by the New Zealand drivers' association to compete in Europe. Among those who discovered his potential was Jack Brabham. McLaren arrived in England in 1958 with his friend and mechanic, Colin Beanland. There, he caught the attention of Charles and John Cooper, who gave him a Formula 2 car. In his debut at the German Grand Prix at the Nürburgring, McLaren impressed by finishing fifth overall. At just twenty years old, on one of the world's most challenging tracks, this feat demonstrated exceptional skill. Later recruited by Ken Tyrrell, McLaren raced for his Cooper team in the junior categories, which served as an excellent foundation for his career. Paired with Jack Brabham, McLaren won his first Formula 1 Grand Prix at Sebring in the United States at the end of 1959. At just twenty-two years old, he became the youngest Grand Prix winner, a record held until Alonso broke it in 2003 by less than eighty days. With Cooper, McLaren added wins at the 1960 Argentine Grand Prix and the 1962 Monaco Grand Prix. He remained with the team after Brabham left to become a constructor, also competing in prototype cars. His most significant achievement came at the 1966 24 Hours of Le Mans, where he and fellow New Zealander Chris Amon won in a Ford GT40. By the end of 1959, McLaren met Patricia Broad, known as Pat, whom he married. They had a daughter, Amanda, born in November 1965. Like Jack Brabham, McLaren balanced family life, the garage, and the racetrack.

In addition to four Formula 1 Grand Prix victories, Bruce McLaren won the 1966 24 Hours of Le Mans with a Ford GT40, paired with Chris Amon.

BRUCE McLAREN *AUCKLAND 08-20-1937*
GOODWOOD CIRCUIT 06-02-1970

GP ENTERED	*100*
F1 WINS	*4*

Following Brabham's example, McLaren began laying the groundwork for his own team in 1964 by competing in the Tasman Cup with modified Coopers. The series proved successful, though tragic, as young American teammate Timmy Mayer died in a crash. Along with Mayer's brother Teddy and Tyler Alexander, McLaren founded his team, which announced its Formula 1 entry at the end of 1965. From that point, McLaren transformed into a test driver, designer, and occasional inventor, introducing innovations like the "nostril" air intakes. Successes poured in from the Can-Am series, which featured sports cars powered by production-derived engines racing in the United States and Canada. McLaren cars dominated the Can-Am championships of 1967, 1968, and 1969, with wins by Bruce, Denis Hulme, and McLaren himself. In Formula 1, Bruce secured his team's first victory at the 1968 Belgian Grand Prix at Spa. To date, he remains the only driver, alongside Jack Brabham, to win a Grand Prix in a car of his own design. Denis Hulme, who had joined his fellow New Zealander's team that year as the reigning World Champion, added wins in the Italian and Canadian Grand Prix. In 1970, while continuing to compete in Formula 1, Bruce focused on developing the car for the Can-Am championship, which kicked off in mid-June. The new M8D was ready for testing in England, and on June 2, McLaren headed to Goodwood to try it out. While running at about 167.7 mph (270 km/h), the rear hood suddenly lifted, causing the car to lose stability and crash into a marshal's hut on the side of the track. McLaren didn't stand a chance—he died instantly, leaving an irreplaceable void in his family, his company, and the entire world of motorsport. Despite his loss, the M8D dominated the Can-Am series with Denis Hulme behind the wheel. Meanwhile, McLaren's Formula 1 team was gearing up for its big breakthrough, which came in the 1970s with World Championship titles won by Emerson Fittipaldi and James Hunt—not to mention their legendary victories at the Indianapolis 500 in 1972, 1974, and 1976.

The 1970 Spanish Grand Prix at Jarama was McLaren's penultimate race. Driving a car of his own design, the New Zealander finished second behind Stewart.

HINCHMAN
ESSO
Graham Hill.

GRAHAM HILL

Born in Hampstead, London, in 1929, Graham Hill was one of the most colorful characters among the hundreds of figures who have shaped motorsport since its inception. Distinguished by his mustache, neatly combed hair, and quintessentially British composure, he was instantly recognizable. Hill's sharp sense of humor and generosity toward journalists made him a popular figure, alongside a career brimming with victories. His father was a stockbroker, though money was often tight, a situation that worsened with the outbreak of World War II. At sixteen, Hill began working in a factory that produced musical instruments. At twenty-one, he enlisted in the Navy, and at twenty-three, upon his return, he joined the London Rowing Club, whose crest would later become the iconic symbol on his racing helmet. As for cars, he had to wait until he was twenty-four to get one. It was a 1929 Austin as old as he was, a jalopy he bought for a few pounds.

His passion for cars and speed skyrocketed when he took laps at Brands Hatch in a Formula 3 single-seater provided by a racing school, where he later became an instructor for meager pay. Hill's fortunes changed when he met Colin Chapman, founder of Lotus. Initially hired as a mechanic for one pound a day, Hill convinced Chapman to let him race, eventually finding himself behind the wheel of a Lotus Formula 1 car at the 1958 Monaco Grand Prix. Meanwhile, in 1955, Hill married Bette, who would become an institution in the British motorsport world and mother to his three children: Brigitte, Samantha, and Damon, Graham's only son.

Hill's early years at Lotus were challenging, marred by frequent retirements and few notable finishes. In 1960, he moved to Louis Stanley's BRM, a team struggling for respectability, which at that time was not achieving prestigious results. Hill's unyielding determination and optimism transformed BRM's fortunes. In 1962, he won his first Grand Prix in Zandvoort, Netherlands, followed by victories in Germany, Italy, and South Africa, earning his first World Championship title. BRM was at the top of its game, though Hill had to give way to Clark and his Lotus in 1963, finishing second the following year behind John Surtees, who won the World Championship with Ferrari. In the decisive race in Mexico, Graham Hill was hit by Bandini's Ferrari, Surtees's teammate, forcing him to retire. In more recent times, such an incident would have sparked endless controversy, but Hill responded with his trademark humor, sending Lorenzo Bandini a Christmas gift of records containing a complete course on how to drive a car. Over the next two years, he found himself teamed with rising star Jackie Stewart, though Hill still managed to finish as runner-up in the 1965 championship, behind Clark.

By then, Hill had become a household name, known for his

Graham Hill won World Championships in 1962 and 1968 before founding a team named after him.

GRAHAM HILL	HAMPSTEAD 02-15-1929 ARKLEY 11-29-1975
GP ENTERED	176
F1 WINS	14
POLE POSITIONS	13
F1 WORLD CHAMPIONSHIPS	1962, 1968

jovial personality and love of life. Despite a busy family life, he was famous for partying, joking, and even dancing on tables. With the money he earned, he purchased a private plane to travel across Europe, though passengers often described his flights as "not the safest." Meanwhile, BRM was losing its edge, and despite the prestigious and lucrative victory at the 1966 Indianapolis 500, Hill returned to Lotus in 1967, teaming up with Jim Clark. The Lotus 49, powered by a Ford engine, was incredibly fast but only won with Clark, who still lost the 1967 championship to Hulme driving for Brabham. When the Scottish champion tragically lost his life in a Formula 2 crash at the start of 1968, Hill became the Lotus team leader. With three victories, he narrowly defeated Jackie Stewart and his Matra at the final Grand Prix in Mexico, securing his second World Championship. In 1969, Hill was paired with a new and challenging teammate, Jochen Rindt, and achieved his fifth victory at Monte Carlo. However, his career took a downward turn following a severe crash at Watkins Glen (United States), during the penultimate Grand Prix of the year, leaving him with a broken leg. In 1970, he joined Rob Walker's private team, which competed with the Lotus 72, and then moved to Brabham for the next two seasons. Despite declining performance—due to his age and the lingering effects of the crash—in 1972 he claimed a career milestone by winning the 24 Hours of Le Mans in a Matra alongside Henri Pescarolo.

In 1973, Hill founded his own team, first racing with Lola cars and later constructing his own chassis starting in 1975. That same year, after failing to qualify for the Monaco Grand Prix, he announced his retirement. Graham Hill had discovered a promising young talent, Tony Brise, who had already scored the first points for the Hill team and was widely tipped for a bright future.

Tragically, their story came to a sudden end on the evening of November 29, 1975. Hill was piloting his Piper Aztec on the return flight from a testing session at Le Castellet in southern France. Despite the darkness and heavy fog, he attempted to land at Elstree, where his car was parked. The plane crashed, killing Hill, Tony Brise, and four other team members. Hill's legacy lived on through his son, Damon, who won the 1996 Formula 1 World Championship with Williams.

A view of the starting grid at the 1968 French Grand Prix in Rouen, with Graham Hill's unmistakable helmet in the foreground

JIM CLARK

Jim Clark came from a wealthy family of sheep farmers in Edington Mains, near Kilmany, where he was born in 1936. The youngest of five children and the only boy, he was expected to inherit and manage the family business. Using this as leverage, Clark persuaded his father to let him leave school at sixteen. By eighteen, he was already driving his Sunbeam-Talbot in clandestine gymkhanas and rallies. Despite opposition from his family, Clark joined the amateur racing team Border Reivers, where his exceptional talent quickly became apparent. In 1957, driving a Porsche 356 purchased by his friend Ian Scott-Watson, Clark won three of the five races he entered. His success continued with a Jaguar D-Type and more victories in 1958, driving Lister Jaguars and Lotus Elites. Gifted with extraordinary natural talent, he quickly rose to prominence. He was so skilled that his friend Ian Scott-Watson bought him a Porsche 356, with which he won three of the five races he entered at the end of 1957. His star kept rising with a Jaguar D-Type and Porsche for Border Reivers, winning most of the races he entered in 1958, and success continued the following year with a Lister Jaguar and a Lotus Elite.

Colin Chapman, the visionary founder of Lotus, took notice and signed Clark for Formula Junior in 1960 after a test at Goodwood, where Clark shattered the track record by four seconds. By early June, he was already on the grid for the Dutch Grand Prix, driving a Lotus 18 and holding fifth place until he was forced to retire. The tragedy of the subsequent Belgian Grand Prix at Spa, marked by the fatal accidents of Stacey in a Lotus and Bristow in a Cooper, as well as crashes involving Moss and Taylor in their Lotus cars, nearly convinced Clark to quit racing. However, Chapman persuaded him to continue, and Clark soon emerged as a rising star in Formula 1. On September 10, 1961, at Monza, Clark unintentionally triggered one of motorsport's most horrific accidents. The lightweight Lotus he was driving allowed him to brake later than other cars, and as he entered the Parabolica curve, he clipped the exhausts of von Trips's Ferrari, which veered into the crowd before flipping over the other cars. The German driver was killed, along with fourteen spectators. Devastated, Clark returned home only to find photographers waiting to snap pictures, adding to his anguish.

Off the track, Jim was a reserved person who avoided publicity and hated the spotlight, though he was always available to journalists and photographers at races. In contrast to his analytical and decisive driving style, he was famously indecisive in daily life, struggling to choose restaurants or movies. Nervous before races, he bit his nails, a habit he justified by saying it was better

A striking portrait of Jim Clark, a purebred Scot and a driver of extraordinary class, rightly considered the best of his era

JIM CLARK — *KILMANY 03-04-1936* / *HOCKENHEIM 04-07-1968*

GP ENTERED	*72*
F1 WINS	*25*
POLE POSITIONS	*33*
F1 WORLD CHAMPIONSHIPS	*1963, 1965*

DUNLOP

than smoking. Jim had an exceptional ability to push any car to its limits. In an era when the machine had not yet entirely overshadowed the driver, he almost always excelled in all categories and on any type of track. Despite his unparalleled skill in mastering mechanical vehicles, he was often quite nervous before races. He disliked driving in the middle of a pack and always tried to distance himself from the group. He feared the overly aggressive competitiveness of some rivals, though he himself always showed the utmost fairness to those he raced against.

After overcoming the trauma of the Monza crash, Clark began dominating with the Lotus 25, Formula 1's first monocoque car, which he drove in a semi-reclined position with outstretched arms. He claimed victories in Belgium, England, and the United States, but too many retirements prevented him from securing the title. He succeeded in 1963, dominating the championship by winning seven out of ten Grands Prix. Dubbed "The Flying Scotsman," Clark became a global icon. In 1964, his Lotus let him down too often, but the following year, with the new 33,

Left: In 1964, Clark missed out on the World Championship but triumphed at the Belgian Grand Prix, as seen here on the podium at Spa-Francorchamps.

Above: The flamboyant marshal at Watkins Glen waves the checkered flag as Jim Clark claims victory at the 1967 United States Grand Prix.

he became unstoppable again, winning six out of ten Grands Prix. That same year, he added the prestigious Indianapolis 500 to his achievements. The 1966 regulation changes hampered Lotus, allowing Jim to secure only one victory, in the United States, after switching engines from BRM to Climax. Redemption came with the Lotus 49 and its revolutionary Ford V8 engine, but frequent retirements cost him the 1967 championship, which went to Hulme with Brabham. Nonetheless, Clark claimed memorable victories in the Netherlands, Great Britain, the United States, and Mexico. At Monza, he staged one of Formula 1's greatest comebacks, recovering a ninety-second deficit after a pit stop. Unfortunately, he ran out of fuel just short of victory, at the end of a chase that everyone had believed impossible. Toward the end of his career, Clark appeared more relaxed and content. He had become engaged to Sally Stokes, a model he planned to marry after retiring from racing. Jim Clark's legend continued with another victory at the 1968 South African Grand Prix in Kyalami, held on New Year's Day. Tragically, his career and life ended abruptly on April 7, 1968, during a Formula 2 race at Hockenheim. Traveling at over 149 mph (240 km/h), his Lotus veered off the track and crashed into the woods. Clark died instantly. A tire failure was suspected, but the exact cause of the accident remains unknown. Nevertheless, everyone agreed that the mistake was certainly not his.

Above: On April 7, 1968, Clark prepares for the start of a Formula 2 race at Hockenheim, where he was involved in an infamous accident that cost his life.

Right: Clark in the cockpit of teammate Peter Arundell's Lotus at Zandvoort in 1966, comparing its BRM engine with the Climax in his single-seater car.

8
TEAM LOTUS
8

JOHN SURTEES

John Surtees, the only man to become a World Champion on both two and four wheels was born in Tatsfield, Surrey, in 1934. His father, Jack, was a motorcycle salesman and racing enthusiast who, in 1949, entered a competition with John sitting in the sidecar. Although he won, Jack was disqualified because his son didn't have a license. By age sixteen, John was ready to race solo and began competing regularly after being hired by Vincent, a motorcycle manufacturer. Without hesitation, he made a name for himself before turning eighteen, boldly taking on established champions like Geoff Duke. In 1955, Surtees joined Norton's official team, winning an impressive sixty-eight out of the seventy-six races. The following year, he moved to MV Agusta, where he stayed from 1956 to 1960. These golden years brought three World Championships in the 350cc class and four in the 500cc category, including prestigious victories at the feared Isle of Man TT. Italians began calling him "figlio del vento" (son of the wind), a nickname that stuck, while the English simply referred to him as "Big John."

While speeding on motorcycles, Surtees wanted to experience the thrill of racing cars, encouraged by Mike Hawthorn and other British drivers. After testing Ken Tyrrell's Formula Junior Cooper, he debuted in March 1960 at Goodwood, finishing second only to Jim Clark in his Lotus. Colin Chapman was so impressed that he offered Surtees an official Lotus car for four Grands Prix that didn't conflict with his motorcycle commitments. After a modest debut at Monaco, Surtees finished second at Silverstone and was highly competitive in Portugal, where he led until retiring, and in the United States. After stepping away from motorcycle racing, Surtees became a full-time Formula 1 driver in 1961 and 1962, competing for Cooper and Lola. A pair of second-place finishes at Rouen and Aintree in Eric Broadley's Lola raised his profile, leading to a pivotal call from Maranello in 1963. Enzo Ferrari had always admired British motorcycle racers and drivers, as well as Surtees's combative spirit on two wheels. After meeting him, Ferrari appreciated Surtees's meticulous approach to race preparation and vehicle mechanics. The Maranello cars regained competitiveness in 1963 despite Lotus and Jim Clark's dominance. A victory at the Nürburgring, Maranello's first in nearly two years, proved crucial. In 1964, Surtees found himself in contention for the title after victories at Nürburgring and Monza. At the decisive Mexican Grand Prix, teammate Lorenzo Bandini helped Surtees by yielding second place late in the race. The Italian driver had also unintentionally collided with Graham Hill, ending his title hopes. Thus, John Surtees became the first—and still only—man to win World Championships both on motorcycles and in Formula 1.

Surtees's excellent relationship with Ferrari began to fray

John Surtees remains the only person to win World Championships in both motorcycle racing and Formula 1, the latter with Ferrari in 1964.

JOHN SURTEES — *TATSFIELD 02-11-1934* / *LONDON 03-10-2017*

GP ENTERED	*111*
F1 WINS	*6*
POLE POSITIONS	*8*
F1 WORLD CHAMPIONSHIPS	*1964*

the following year, when he raced for Lola in the Can-Am series. Tensions worsened after a severe crash at Mosport in late September forced him to miss two Formula 1 Grands Prix. With his left leg shortened by about 0.8 inches (two centimeters), he spent six months recovering but was ready for the new season.

At Ferrari, Surtees clashed with team manager Eugenio Dragoni, who strongly favored Bandini. Despite winning the Belgian Grand Prix in 1966, tensions persisted, and on the eve of the 24 Hours of Le Mans, Surtees left Ferrari to race with Cooper in Formula 1 and Lola in Can-Am. His decision wasn't without success, as

he won the Can-Am championship and finished second in the Formula 1 World Championship, thanks to a second-place finish at Nürburgring and a remarkable victory in Mexico. The Ferrari split was later deemed a mistake by both sides. Ferrari was certainly not an easy personality to deal with, but Surtees was equally unwilling to compromise on his pride and impulsiveness. If he had something to say, he wouldn't mince words, often being direct to the point of verbal aggression. It was a flaw he himself acknowledged in his later years.

Surtees's career continued with Honda in 1967, where he achieved a memorable victory at the Italian Grand Prix, followed by a stint with BRM in 1969. In 1970, he launched his own team, becoming a constructor and racing personally until 1972. His greatest success came in the 1972 European Formula 2 Championship, won by Mike Hailwood, another motorcycle champion turned car racer. After disbanding his team and construction activities in 1978, Surtees retired to manage a motorcycle shop and a Honda dealership. Following an initial childless marriage, he remarried and had three children, two daughters and a son. His youngest, Henry, showed great potential as a driver but tragically died at just eighteen after being struck by a tire during a Formula 2 race in July 2009. For Sir John Surtees, this loss was his greatest sorrow, motivating him to establish a foundation in Henry's memory.

Left: In the final phase of his career, Surtees founded his own team. Here he drives a McLaren at Zandvoort in 1970 before debuting in a single-seater of his own design.

Above: The reigning World Champion driving the Ferrari 158 during practice for the 1965 British Grand Prix at Silverstone

DUNLOP

LORENZO BANDINI

Lorenzo Bandini was admired by many, if not everyone, for his simple and kind demeanor—a typical good guy who had achieved his dream despite an entirely unfavorable start in life. He was born in Barce, Libya, in December 1935 to a family of Italian emigrants, and his father, Giovanni, was executed during World War II after returning to Italy, though the family only discovered this later. These events plunged the family into severe hardship. Lorenzo grew up in Reggiolo, a small town near Reggio Emilia, and started working in a machine shop at a young age. In 1950, feeling ready for the big city, he moved to Milan, where his sister Gabriella lived. He found a job at the Rex garage owned by Goliardo Freddi. A romance blossomed between Lorenzo and Margherita, the garage owner's daughter, and Freddi became a father figure to Bandini, supporting his dream of becoming a racing driver. Bandini debuted in 1956 at a hill climb in Castell'Arquato, driving a Fiat 1100 TV lent to him by Margherita. His passion for racing took over completely, and he moved on to a more advanced Fiat V8 coupe. At the 1958 Mille Miglia, he won his class with a Lancia Appia, beginning to make a name for himself. He also competed in Formula Junior, first as a privateer in 1959 and then as an official Stanguellini driver in 1960, winning the Cuban Grand Prix at Camp Freedom.

Meanwhile, the Italian Federation of Auto Racing Teams (FISA) secured an opportunity for a young driver to race a Formula 1 car for Ferrari. Though Bandini had hoped to be selected, the spot went to Giancarlo Baghetti. However, Bandini's disappointment was quickly mitigated when Mimmo Dei's Scuderia Centro Sud signed him to race a Cooper-Maserati car. His Formula 1 debut came at the Pau Grand Prix, where he finished third behind Clark and Bonnier. More importantly, he won the Pescara 4 Hours in a Ferrari Testa Rossa, alongside Giorgio Scarlatti, which earned him a spot on the official team. Although Ferrari only had him race three World Championship Grands Prix, including Monaco, where he finished third, Bandini also claimed victory at Pergusa. In 1963, he was forced to settle for a Centro Sud BRM, resulting in limited Formula 1 appearances. However, other successes followed: After marrying Margherita in February, Lorenzo won the 24 Hours of Le Mans with Ludovico Scarfiotti and ended the year as the Italian Champion.

Returning to Ferrari for Formula 1 too, Bandini, paired with John Surtees, drove the excellent Ferrari 158 to victory at the 1964 Austrian Grand Prix in Zeltweg. At the season's decisive race in Mexico City, Bandini's assistance was crucial in helping Surtees secure the championship.

Everything seemed to be heading in the right direction, especially with his victory at the 1965 Targa Florio alongside Vaccarella and his second-place finish at the Monaco Grand Prix. However,

The driver with his wife, Margherita, who served as his timekeeper, during practice for the 1966 Italian Grand Prix.

LORENZO BANDINI | *BARCE 12-21-1935*
MONTE CARLO 05-10-1967

GP ENTERED	*42*
F1 WINS	*1*
POLE POSITIONS	*1*

further victories eluded him, and tensions arose within Ferrari as Surtees remained the team's top driver. In 1966, after Surtees's contentious departure from Ferrari, Bandini finished second again at Monaco but was not promoted to the lead driver position. Things changed at the start of 1967, when Ferrari finally decided to bet on Lorenzo, pairing him with young Chris Amon instead of Ludovico Scarfiotti, whom Bandini could barely tolerate. Now mature and polished, he focused on both his image and the meticulous tuning of his cars. He was always impeccably dressed and groomed—photos from that era show how elegant he was—but he never forgot his past as a mechanic, forming strong friendships with the team's crew. With an improved contract, he purchased a property in Brisighella to retire with his beloved Margherita, nicknamed Giò. Though he lacked Jim Clark's natural talent, Bandini was an excellent test driver who dreamed of winning the World Championship. His 1967 season began well, with wins in the 24 Hours of Daytona and the 1,000 km of Monza with Ferrari's 330 P4.

Then came the Monaco Grand Prix in early May. Bandini was so confident that he asked his wife to join him on Thursday and bring a tuxedo to attend the royal reception in case of victory. At the start, everything seemed to go perfectly. Bandini outpaced Brabham, who was on pole position, and took the lead. However, Brabham's engine failed shortly afterward, and the unlucky Italian driver was the first to run over the debris on the following lap. Spinning out, he found himself behind Hulme, who had taken the lead in the other Brabham. The heat and the strain of a difficult comeback, with the gap stubbornly refusing to close, began to take their toll. Midway through the race, Bandini was visibly exhausted, his upper body swaying unsteadily inside the cockpit, which still lacked seat belts. On the eighty-second lap, after more than two hours of racing, tragedy struck. Bandini's Ferrari hit the wooden barriers at the harbor chicane, hit a mooring bollard, and flipped over, catching fire. Trapped under the car for three and a half minutes, he was finally pulled out. The horrifying scene haunted those who witnessed it, both live and on television. Severely burned, Bandini succumbed to his injuries three days later at the Monte Carlo hospital.

Left: Bandini leading with his Ferrari 1512 at the 1965 Monaco Grand Prix. He ultimately finished second behind Graham Hill's BRM.

Right: One of the last images of Lorenzo Bandini in the front row at the 1967 Monaco Grand Prix, where he suffered a fatal accident during the eighty-second lap

GIANCARLO BAGHETTI

Giancarlo Baghetti is not as well known as Fangio, Clark, Stewart, or Senna, yet he set a record that will likely remain unbroken in Formula 1 history. He is, in fact, the only driver ever to win a World Championship Grand Prix on his debut. On July 4, 1961, a handsome young Milanese climbed to the top step of the podium after narrowly outpacing Dan Gurney's Porsche in a photo finish. That remarkable victory is matched only by Baghetti's equally incredible backstory. Born on Christmas Day 1934 into a wealthy family of steel industrialists, he dreamed of driving from a very early age. He was so convincing that his father had a special car built for him, which he could drive around the family estates.

Racing seemed like a natural progression, and by falsifying his ID, Baghetti debuted on a Lambretta at just thirteen. By sixteen, he already had his own car, which he drove on public roads without a license. Known to local police, who assumed he was of age, he regularly escaped trouble. Despite their own passion for motorsport, his parents forbade him from racing. At twenty-one, Baghetti owned a Lancia Aurelia, unsuitable for racing, but an Alfa Romeo 1900 TI in the family garage was perfect for the job. At night, Giancarlo secretly took it to a mechanic, Luigi Dagrada, who prepared it for competition. After a few weeks of clandestine tuning, with his father growing increasingly amazed at how much faster his car seemed to be every day, Baghetti debuted at Monza, leading until an engine failure. Once the secret was discovered, instead of being punished, he was gifted a Giulietta Sprint Veloce, which he used to start racing. Dagrada, the mechanic and accomplice, directly funded the young man's racing activities, getting reimbursed at the end of the year after heated discussions with Baghetti's father. This happened between 1956 and 1959, before Giancarlo moved to Formula Junior with a single-seater designed, of course, by Dagrada. In 1959, alongside competing with that car, he was hired as an official driver for Abarth, setting numerous speed records with the team. The turning point came in 1960, when Baghetti excelled in Formula Junior and won the FISA Cup, earning him the opportunity to drive a Formula 1 Ferrari designated for young Italian drivers. Although fitted with the previous year's engine, it was still a highly competitive car, and Baghetti didn't waste the chance. He won on his debut at the non-championship Grand Prix of Syracuse, stunning everyone by beating the best British drivers of the time, including Moss and Clark, as well as the Porsche duo of Gurney and Bonnier, who finished behind him. He repeated his success at the Grand Prix of Naples in Posillipo, perhaps without fully realizing the significance of these victories.

In July, Ferrari finally entered him in the French Grand Prix. On a scorching day at the high-speed Reims circuit, Baghetti kept his cool during a nail-biting duel with Gurney's Porsche. With a clever feint left and a decisive move right, he edged past his rival to win by just 20 inches (50 centimeters). In Italy, he became a sensation almost overnight. When he returned to Maranello a few days later, Enzo Ferrari famously asked him if he remembered which car he had won with. Even Ferrari acknowledged Baghetti's smooth driving style, attributing it to his innate talent behind the wheel, and went so far as to compare him to Achille Varzi, the ultimate refined driver of the heroic era of racing. Baghetti's meteoric rise placed him among the brightest young talents of 1961, alongside Jim Clark. Together with the Scotsman, he witnessed the Monza tragedy up close, as von Trips's Ferrari flew into the crowd, narrowly missing him as it came crashing down.

Looking back after all these years, it's astonishing how Baghetti's career at the top was so short-lived. The decline of Ferrari's competitiveness in 1962 and his ill-fated move to ATS in 1963 hastened his fall from grace. His final Formula 1 season came in 1964 with Centro Sud's BRM, followed by sporadic competitions in the Italian Grand Prix until 1967. He continued racing in sports and touring cars, occasionally achieving respectable results. Many believe that, due to his privileged upbringing and carefree childhood, he was ill-prepared to handle adversity effectively. Even he admitted that the lack of competitive cars prevented him from fully realizing his potential, as he was often left battling for lesser positions. His impeccable manners, while endearing, may have worked against him in a cutthroat sport that rewards aggressiveness. As a driver, he knew how to enjoy life, taking advantage of the fact that many beautiful women followed the races. He could be described as a playboy, though he sometimes preferred to spend the Saturday before a race alone, staying calm and focused.

Baghetti was present at Monte Carlo during Lorenzo Bandini's tragic accident and was among those who tried to pull the stricken driver from the burning car. Just over a year later, during the Formula 2 Lotteria Grand Prix at Monza, Jean-Pierre Jaussaud's car flew over Baghetti's head in a horrifying crash. Shaken, Baghetti returned to the pits and announced his retirement. It was June 1968. He later married Cristina Vianini, sister of Argentinian driver Andrea, and had a beloved son named Aaron. After stepping away from racing, he became a journalist and photographer, occasionally participating in rallies and endurance events with production cars. Sadly, he passed away in 1995 after a brief illness, leaving the motorsport world mourning the loss of a true gentleman.

The Milanese driver Baghetti remains the only person to win a Formula 1 Grand Prix on debut, at the 1961 French Grand Prix in Reims.

GIANCARLO BAGHETTI *MILAN 12-25-1934*
MILAN 11-27-1995

GP ENTERED 21
F1 WINS 1

JACKIE STEWART

In his school days, he was simply known as John Young, and he faced difficult times, later described as the hardest of his life. The man who would become Jackie Stewart was, in fact, a dyslexic child and could not continue secondary school beyond the age of sixteen. His parents ran a car dealership in Milton, Scotland, and his brother Jimmy had raced with decent success, even participating in the 1953 British Grand Prix. For young Jackie, born in June 1939, redemption from the disappointments of school came quickly. He possessed extraordinary hand-eye coordination and discovered his exceptional shooting ability at thirteen. His career as a clay shooter took him to great heights, and he was so skilled that he nearly made the British national team for the 1960 Rome Olympics. Stewart worked with his parents and was also a highly competent driver, to the point that he was given the opportunity to test a customer's racing cars at Oulton Park. The test went excellently, but convincing his family, especially his mother, was not easy, considering Jimmy had suffered a terrible accident at Le Mans. Jackie started making a name for himself with Barry Filer's cars, a customer of the family garage. During this period, he met Helen McGregor, whose parents owned a bakery in the city. They got along so well that after two years, in 1962, they married. Their marriage would go on to become one of the happiest of all time, and they were later blessed with children Mark and Paul.

Signed by Ecurie Ecosse in 1963, Jackie continued winning with various cars until the end of the year, when he was called to Goodwood to test Ken Tyrrell's new Formula 3 Cooper. He was immediately faster than the experienced Bruce McLaren, who returned to the track to improve his time. He managed to do so, but once again, Stewart outshone him, earning the spot to race in the 1964 British Formula 3 Championship. This began his partnership with one of the greatest talent scouts of all time. The season was triumphant, with seven victories in ten races. By 1965, Stewart was already racing in Formula 1 with BRM, alongside the experienced Graham Hill. It was no surprise when he was immediately one of the best, securing several prestigious podiums and eventually winning his first Grand Prix at Monza, finishing ahead of Hill. The following year, he won in Monte Carlo and was poised to triumph in the Indianapolis 500 but was betrayed by a fuel system failure just eight laps from the end.

Then came the breakthrough at the 1966 Belgian Grand Prix at Spa. Stewart went off-track in his BRM due to a sudden downpour at the Masta Esses and found himself trapped in the car with the chassis bent. Fearing a spinal injury, he was relieved that only his collarbone was broken. From that point on, Stewart became a strong advocate for safety, supported by the drivers' association and particularly by his friend Jochen Rindt.

Gifted with immense talent, as a driver Jackie Stewart overcame the challenges that dyslexia posed during his school years.

JACKIE STEWART	*MILTON 11-6-1939*
GP ENTERED	*99*
F1 WINS	*27*
POLE POSITIONS	*17*
F1 WORLD CHAMPIONSHIPS	*1969, 1971, 1973*

Jackie Stewart on the podium at Zandvoort after one of the six victories that led to his first World Championship title in 1969 with Matra-Ford

He campaigned for guardrails, safety barriers, medical assistance, and specialized marshals. His proposals were not always popular, especially since they would require a substantial financial outlay from race organizers. Incredibly, a part of the press suggested that the lack of danger would dull the challenges and make it more difficult to select drivers. The repeated tragedies of the following years ultimately vindicated Stewart, who correctly argued that drivers should be paid for their talent, not for the risks they took. He often joked that no one would ever ask Tom Jones, the popular singer of the time, to be electrocuted by a microphone.

After three years with BRM, it was time for a change. Ken Tyrrell, with whom Stewart had already worked in Formula 2 in 1967, offered him a chance to race. The English manager took charge of Matra's cars, now

Above: The Scottish champion with Grace Kelly and Prince Rainier of Monaco on the podium after winning the 1966 Monaco Grand Prix, driving for BRM

powered by the new Ford V8 engines. Stewart won three Grands Prix, with a legendary victory at the Nürburgring—perhaps the most dangerous track of them all. Under pouring rain, he finished over four minutes ahead of Hill, who came in second. That win in such harsh, dangerous conditions gave more credibility to his safety campaign. Behind the wheel, Stewart had taken up the mantle of his late friend Jim Clark. On the track, he remained calm and composed, with exceptional car control that allowed him to go fast while risking less than others. Off the track, Stewart began to commercialize his image and can be considered the first professional driver of the modern era. He was criticized for this, and also for moving his residence to Switzerland, allegedly for tax reasons. Still, he was always a friend of the British royal family, even before being knighted in 2001. His class took him to the World Championship title in 1969, before Matra decided to manage everything in-house. Tyrrell bought a new March car in 1970, which was virtually undrivable for the time. Yet, Stewart managed to win—the only driver among his teammates with the same car—achieving victory at the Spanish Grand Prix. By the end of the year, the Tyrrell team debuted, starting its victorious era with World Championship titles in 1971 and 1973. Stewart announced his retirement at the end of 1973. The team had already chosen his successor in François Cevert, who tragically lost his life in a crash during practice for the final Grand Prix at Watkins Glen. Jackie retired before the last race, having won twenty-seven Grands Prix out of ninety-nine starts. As a savvy businessman, he found great success later as a TV commentator, consultant, and even owner of a Formula 1 team with his son Paul from 1997 to 1999.

The 1971 Tyrrell 003 driven by Stewart in the Spanish Grand Prix at Montjuïc. It was Jackie's first victory of the season, leading to his World Championship title.

RIND

JOCHEN RINDT

Jochen Rindt holds one of the saddest records in Formula 1 history: He remains the only posthumous World Champion. Widely regarded as one of the strongest drivers of his era, the Austrian's career spanned just about a decade before it was tragically cut short. Born in Mainz, Germany, in 1942, Rindt lost both parents in an air raid on Hamburg when he was just fifteen months old. He was raised by his maternal grandparents in Graz and, luckily enough, could rely on the fortune his family's business left behind. At eighteen, as soon as he could, he began racing in touring cars but quickly transitioned to Formula Junior. In 1963, Rindt arrived at Monte Carlo in style, towing his Cooper behind a sleek Jaguar E-Type while wearing red pants and a pink shirt. That flair caught the eye of Nina Lincoln, a Finnish model and daughter of Curt Lincoln, one of Rindt's rivals at the event. Sparks flew, and Nina soon became his wife.

Rindt was very fast, and his aggressive, fearless driving style quickly gained attention, earning him support from Austrian Ford to debut in Formula 2 in 1964. At Mallory Park, he shocked the field by taking pole and finishing third in the race behind Jim Clark and Peter Arundell. The very next day, he won both the second heat and the final, beating Graham Hill. His sideways driving style thrilled fans, earning cheers and applause from the crowd. That same year, he made his Formula 1 debut at the Austrian Grand Prix in Zeltweg. By 1965, Rindt became a full-time Formula 1 driver with Cooper. However, his standout achievement of the year was at Le Mans, where he won the 24 Hours with Masten Gregory in a Ferrari 250 LM, driving the lion's share of the race.

Rindt's abilities shone again in 1966, when he finished third in the Formula 1 World Championship with a heavy Cooper powered by a Maserati engine. He dominated Formula 2 in 1967, winning eight races, though he didn't score championship points as a senior driver. After a lackluster 1968 season with Brabham, he teamed up with Bernie Ecclestone as his manager and signed with Lotus for 1969. Very mindful of financial management, Rindt never missed an opportunity to boost his income. He and Bernie Ecclestone carefully weighed the pros and cons of a move to Lotus—a team with more fragile and dangerous cars but with greater chances of winning. The fact that he had never stood on the top step of the podium was beginning to weigh heavily on Rindt. His relationship with team boss Colin Chapman was strained, as Rindt's blunt honesty and constant suggestions to improve the car annoyed Chapman. The risks of Lotus became evident early, with a rear-wing failure in Spain sending Rindt into a crash that left him hospitalized with facial injuries and a broken nose. After a few pole positions, some second places, a

Jochen Rindt tragically remains the only World Champion who didn't live to know he had won the title.

JOCHEN RINDT — *MAINZ 04-18-1942* / *MONZA 09-05-1970*

GP ENTERED	*60*
F1 WINS	*6*
POLE POSITIONS	*10*
F1 WORLD CHAMPIONSHIPS	*1970*

Colin Chapman speaks with Rindt, who takes a break in the pits, smoking a cigarette. In the background, Rindt's wife, Nina, times the other drivers on track.

couple of retirements, and a handful of other wins in Formula 2, he claimed his long-awaited first Formula 1 victory at Watkins Glen that year. In 1970, Lotus introduced the revolutionary 72, featuring side-mounted radiators and a wedge-shaped nose. It was supposed to be the winning weapon of the season, but Rindt couldn't use it right away, and to win at Monaco with the older 49, he had to capitalize on a last-corner mistake by Jack Brabham. Once equipped with the 72, Rindt was unstoppable, winning in the Netherlands, France, Britain, and Germany. The Dutch Grand Prix was marred by the death of Piers Courage, one of Rindt's closest friends, further fueling his growing discomfort with the sport's dangers. Heading into Monza, Rindt had hinted at retiring after the season, wanting to escape the frequent tragedies of Formula 1 and focus on his infant daugh-

Rindt's first win with the revolutionary Lotus 72 at the 1970 French Grand Prix in Clermont-Ferrand. For the Austrian, it was a year of triumph and tragedy.

ter, Natascha. At the ultra-fast Italian circuit—with an average lap speed of nearly 152 mph (245 km/h)—Lotus decided to remove the wings from the 72 to boost straight-line speed. During Saturday's qualifying, Rindt reached over 174 mph (280 km/h) while braking for the Parabolica corner, oddly positioned on the right side of the track. The Lotus wobbled under braking and suddenly veered left, wedging a wheel between the guardrail and the ground. The car was torn apart on impact, and the accident's severity was worsened by Rindt's habit of not fastening the lower straps of his seatbelt. He wouldn't have survived anyway, but sliding forward, the upper belt cut his jugular. He died almost instantly, unaware that he would be crowned World Champion a few weeks later when his closest rival, Jacky Ickx, failed to surpass his points total.

PIERS COURAGE

Heir to a family dynasty of brewers, Piers Courage was the eldest son of the chairman of Courage Breweries. His passion for racing was sparked during his time at Eton, where he attended high school. It started with a book about Bentley's victory at Le Mans, followed by devouring every motorsport magazine he could find. Back home on Sundays, he would take his mother's Morris and drive it at top speed around the RAF track at Chalgrove. Courage's first step into racing came with a Lotus Seven, financed by his father. However, that was the last financial support he received for his racing career. Firm in his decision to become a professional driver, he chose to fund himself rather than join six generations of Courage family members in the brewing business. True to his name, Piers often pushed the limits on the track, sometimes spinning out as a result. Off the track, he formed friendships with fellow drivers Jonathan Williams and Frank Williams (unrelated). Alongside Jonathan, he co-founded the Anglo-Swiss team to compete in the 1964 European Formula 3 Championship with Lotus cars. A second-place finish at Zandvoort and a third at Reims convinced him to stick with the category for another year. In 1965, he partnered with Frank Williams, driving a Brabham to victories at Silverstone, Goodwood, Caserta, and Reims. At the end of the year, he was personally presented with the Grovewood Award by Jim Clark, recognizing him as the most promising British motorsport talent.

Courage continued in Formula 3 with Lotus, achieving notable wins despite the Brabham cars' dominance. In 1966, he made his Formula 2 debut at the German Grand Prix, where lower-category cars were allowed to fill the grid. Piers could be very fast, but he often pushed too hard and ruined his debut with a crash. In 1967, he joined the BRM team and raced in South Africa and Monaco. At Kyalami, he spun multiple times, and in Monaco, he retired after another off-track excursion. BRM dropped him, forcing Piers to fall back into Formula 2, driving a McLaren for John Coombs's team. He delivered some strong results but also suffered a string of nasty crashes at Pau, Pergusa, and Brands Hatch, often betrayed by his tendency to overdo it. Coombs advised him to quit, but of course, Courage didn't listen. Determined to rebuild his reputation, Courage purchased Coombs's McLaren and competed as a privateer in the Tasman Cup series in early 1968. Over seven races, he avoided incidents, consistently finishing near the front and even winning the final race in wet conditions, ahead of Jim Clark. His performance earned him a recall from BRM to race in Formula 1, while simultaneously competing in Formula 2 with the fledgling team of his old friend Frank Williams.

Piers Courage was well liked by everyone for his outgoing personality, sense of humor, and contagious charm. A cultured individual, he had an interest in literature and music, often relaxing with classical pieces. In 1966, he married Sally Curzon, a blond and captivating model who gave him two sons, Jason and Amos. Sally was a great support, even financially, during the difficult times they faced. To pursue his passion for racing, Piers had to give up his family inheritance. Among his colleagues, he became close friends with Bruce McLaren and especially Jochen Rindt, whom he had known since their Formula 3 days. By 1968, Piers seemed like a transformed driver. With BRM, he secured some solid finishes, highlighted by a fourth place at the Italian Grand Prix in Monza. His friendship with Frank Williams had grown so strong it was almost fraternal. In 1969, to race for Frank's team in Formula 1, Piers even turned down an offer from Lotus. Driving a Brabham for Williams's team, Courage immediately made an impact, finishing second at Monaco, a result he repeated at the penultimate race of the season, the US Grand Prix at Watkins Glen. Apart from an off-track excursion at the Nürburgring, he had a clean and incident-free season. His driving style became more refined, and results followed in Formula 2 as well, again with a Brabham managed by his friend Frank. He secured a couple of third-place finishes and, most notably, a victory at the Mediterranean Grand Prix in Pergusa.

He was later invited to Maranello and offered the opportunity to race for Ferrari in 1970 alongside Jacky Ickx. Meanwhile, Frank Williams, always in search of financial backers, had connected with Alejandro de Tomaso, an Argentine industrialist who had become a constructor of sports cars in Modena. Ferrari was coming off a couple of difficult seasons, and Courage was aware of the struggles his friend Jonathan Williams had faced at Maranello. Ultimately, he chose to race with the de Tomaso team managed by Frank Williams and signed a contract with Alfa Romeo to compete in prototype cars. Unfortunately, the new single-seater turned out to be heavy, slow, and unreliable, falling far short of the standards set by the Brabham he had driven the previous year. Courage failed to finish any of the four Grands Prix leading up to the Dutch Grand Prix in June. At Zandvoort, during the twenty-third lap, Piers was in a promising seventh position when his de Tomaso veered wide exiting a high-speed corner. The car flipped and caught fire—the flames further fueled by magnesium used to lighten the chassis. Courage's helmet was found near the wreckage, indicating it had come off during the crash. Tire marks suggested he had likely been struck on the head by a wheel, possibly killing him before the car caught fire.

Courage had the guts to give up financial security to pursue his greatest passion. He became Frank Williams's first driver.

PIERS COURAGE — *COLCHESTER 05-27-1942*
ZANDVOORT 06-21-1970

GP ENTERED — *27*

JACKY ICKX

Jacky Ickx never won a Formula 1 World Championship, but he is widely regarded as one of the greatest drivers of all time. A versatile talent, he excelled in touring cars, Grand Prix single-seaters, the 24 Hours of Le Mans, and even the Paris-Dakar Rally. Born Jacques Bernard Ickx on January 1, 1945, in Brussels, Jacky was the son of a well-known Belgian journalist who covered motorsport and often brought him along to races. His career began with a Zündapp 50 motorcycle, a gift that kick-started his participation in trial events. Success came quickly—he won the Belgian Championship three times before switching to four wheels in 1965, driving a Lotus Cortina. At twenty-one, he claimed victory at the prestigious 24 Hours of Spa, partnering with Hubert Hahne in a BMW, and began competing in sports car events. Ken Tyrrell noticed his talent and recruited him to drive Formula 2 Matras shortly after launching the career of Jackie Stewart. That same year, Ickx made his Formula 1 debut with Matra at the Nürburgring, as junior-category cars were often added to Grand Prix grids to fill out the lineup. The practice continued in Germany the following year, and in 1967, Ickx showcased his skills by qualifying third in the little Matra at the Nürburgring. During the race, he climbed from seventeenth to fourth before retiring. Later, at Monza, Ickx was handed a Cooper-Maserati and finished sixth, catching the attention of Enzo Ferrari, who signed him soon after.

In his debut with Ferrari, he claimed victory at the French Grand Prix in Rouen, a rain-soaked race overshadowed by Jo Schlesser's fatal crash. Meanwhile, he raced John Wyer's Ford GT40 in endurance events, securing wins at Brands Hatch, Spa, Watkins Glen, and Kyalami. Even then, Ickx displayed an independent, almost rebellious streak, refusing to align with Stewart and Rindt when they became vocal advocates for safety. In later years, he admitted that, like many, he believed that accidents could never happen to him. However, Ickx was not indifferent to the issue of safety. At the 1969 24 Hours of Le Mans, drivers were still required to run across the track to their cars, climb in, fire up the engine, and speed off—often without fastening their seat belts. In a dramatic gesture, Ickx calmly walked across the starting grid, got into his GT40, buckled his seat belt, and began the race in last place. That edition of Le Mans became legendary thanks to Ickx's incredible comeback, culminating in a final-lap duel where he overtook Hans Herrmann's Porsche to secure victory. Partnered with Jackie Oliver, Ickx claimed the first of his six wins at Le Mans. From the following year, the traditional running start—known as the "Le Mans-style start"—was abolished.

In Formula 1, he moved to Brabham and won the German and Canadian Grands Prix in 1969. In 1970, he returned to Ferrari to compete in both Formula 1 and sports car racing. After Rindt's tragic death at Monza, Ickx became the only driver capable of challenging the Austrian for the title. However, he almost felt relieved when a

Jacky Ickx flashes a smile after winning the 1969 24 Hours of Le Mans. A versatile driver, he also excelled in the Paris-Dakar Rally.

JACKY ICKX *BRUSSELS 01-01-1945*

GP ENTERED	*114*
F1 WINS	*8*
POLE POSITIONS	*13*

The uncompetitive Wolf-Williams FW05, which the Belgian drove in four Grands Prix in 1976. His Formula 1 career was already on the decline.

fuel issue forced him to retire at Watkins Glen. Little did he know it would be his last chance to become World Champion. Despite a stellar 1972 season with prototype cars, which earned Ferrari the World Championship, tensions with the team grew. Victories at Zandvoort in 1971 and the Nürburgring in 1972 weren't enough to smooth things over. Ickx loved racing above all else, and sometimes when Ferrari summoned him for testing, he sent medical certificates to justify his absences. His rebellious behavior earned him the nickname "pierino la peste" (little rascal) at Ferrari. During this period, he married Catherine Blaton, a wealthy Belgian and the daughter of a construction magnate.

Ferrari's poor performance in 1973 culminated in Ickx skipping the German Grand Prix, opting instead to drive a McLaren. This marked the beginning of the end of his relationship with the Modena-based team. By 1974, he joined Lotus alongside Ronnie Peterson but managed only a single non-championship win at Brands Hatch in wet conditions and a third-place finish at the British Grand Prix. The 1975 season with Lotus was disastrous, and in 1976, Jacky moved to Wolf-Williams before settling with Ensign. However, his time there ended with a broken ankle after a crash at Watkins Glen in the final race of the year. Things went much better in sports cars, where Ickx enjoyed tremendous success, including a spectacular triple victory at the 24 Hours of Le Mans from 1975 to 1977.

Six of Ickx's eight Formula 1 victories were with Ferrari, including his final win at the 1972 German Grand Prix at the Nürburgring.

He triumphed alongside Derek Bell with Mirage before repeating his success with Porsche, first with van Lennep and then with Barth and Haywood. In 1979, when Patrick Depailler broke his legs in a hang gliding accident, Ickx was called to replace him at Ligier, one of the top cars of the time.

However, the ground-effect cars didn't suit the Belgian's precise driving style, and he managed only a couple of finishes before officially retiring from Formula 1. However, he continued to shine in endurance racing. In 1979, he won the Can-Am championship with a Lola. In 1981, he claimed his fifth victory at the 24 Hours of Le Mans with Porsche, paired with Derek Bell—a success the duo repeated the following year. That season also saw Ickx crowned World Endurance Champion after additional wins at Spa, Fuji, and Brands Hatch. He remained with Porsche until 1985, achieving great success, but retired from circuit racing following the tragic death of Stefan Bellof, who crashed while attempting to pass him on the outside of the Raidillon corner during the 1,000 km of Spa-Francorchamps. Ickx then turned his attention to rallying, participating in the Paris-Dakar from 1981 and winning it in 1983 with Mercedes alongside actor Claude Brasseur. More recently, he married African singer Khadja Nin.

He has become more attuned to life's challenges and global issues without losing his deep passion for cars and racing, while also supporting his daughter Vanina's driving career.

FRANÇOIS CEVERT

Widely considered the heartthrob of Formula 1 in the early 1970s, François Cevert was not only blisteringly fast but also a potential champion, ready to step into Jackie Stewart's shoes at Tyrrell in 1974. Cevert took his mother's surname; his father, Charles Goldenberg, was a Jewish jeweler who avoided marrying Cevert's mother during the Nazi occupation to protect his family from persecution. After the war, Goldenberg formally recognized his children, though they kept their mother's name.

François's love for speed began early, racing friends on his Vespa and timing himself between home and school on a Norton motorcycle. While he studied piano at the conservatory and played with impressive skill, his real passion was ignited at the Montlhéry circuit, where he and his sister Jacqueline watched Jean-Pierre Beltoise race motorcycles (Beltoise would soon become engaged to, and later marry, Jacqueline). Cevert's father initially opposed his racing ambitions and cut off financial support until he reached adulthood, after completing his military service. François was engaged to Nanou van Malderen, a divorced noblewoman, when he enrolled in a driving course and went on to win the 1966 "Volant Shell" competition, which promoted young French racing talent. Around this time, Nanou visited a clairvoyant who, as Jacqueline later confirmed, predicted that her fiancé would become famous but wouldn't live to see thirty. Of course, François brushed it off, joking he'd win the World Championship before then. After debuting in Formula 3 in 1967, he went on to become the French champion in the category the following year. In 1969, he was signed to race in Formula 2 with Tecno, where he won a non-championship race at Reims after battling with Jackie Stewart. The Scottish champion and his manager, Ken Tyrrell, took notice of the handsome Frenchman who stood atop the podium. The victory helped ease the pain of his breakup with Nanou, who had faithfully supported him through the tough years, including financially, as François's father, Charles, had cut him off as soon as he started racing.

The turning point in his career came in 1970, when Ken Tyrrell, running March cars in Formula 1, suddenly needed to replace Johnny Servoz-Gavin, who had suffered partial vision loss in one eye following a motocross accident. The young and dashing Parisian couldn't have asked for a better opportunity, coming under the wing of Ken Tyrrell and the patient guidance of a seasoned champion like Jackie Stewart. From the very first laps, the Scottish driver offered plenty of advice and instruction to his young protégé. François had a wonderful personality, in addition to his movie-star looks. Tall, dark haired, and blue eyed, he was a heartthrob who turned heads everywhere he went, though he was romantically involved with Christina de Caraman, a divorced woman of noble origins. The March 701 was a heavy and uncompetitive car, but for Cevert, 1970 was a crucial season. Under Stewart's mentorship, he improved with every race. Driving cleanly and precisely, as the Scotsman advised, he managed to finish in the top six at the Italian Grand Prix at Monza.

In 1971, Tyrell introduced a new car, and the results started pouring in—not just for Stewart, who ended the season as World Champion, but also for Cevert, who claimed his first victory at the United States Grand Prix at Watkins Glen. The win boosted François's morale and his bank account, as he finished the championship in third place. After two seasons, he had become a cherished member of the Tyrrell family. Ken and his wife, Norah, adored him, as did the Stewart family, who treated him like Jackie's younger brother. Women were even more captivated by him, and the French press couldn't resist fueling rumors of a fling with Brigitte Bardot.

Handsome, from a good family, and famous, Cevert was riding high. However, 1972 proved to be a tough year for Tyrrell. Stewart struggled with an ulcer mid-season and adopted a defensive approach, winning only two Grands Prix. Cevert scored points just three times, finishing second in Belgium and once again at Watkins Glen. Things changed dramatically in 1973. The new Tyrrell car, though tricky to drive due to its short wheelbase—better suited to Stewart's clean driving style—proved to be a game changer. Stewart dominated the championship, often with Cevert right behind him, and had already decided to retire at the end of the season. François secured five second-place finishes, and on occasion, even Stewart admitted he could have challenged for the win. But Cevert never seriously considered overtaking his mentor. The final race of the season at Watkins Glen, François's favorite track, was set to be a celebration. During qualifying on October 6, Cevert's Tyrrell lost balance through the fast esses at the start of the circuit, possibly due to an uneven surface. The car veered off-track and flipped over the guardrail, killing Cevert instantly. For those who believe in numerical coincidences, the sequence is haunting: The accident happened on October 6, in car number 6, and he was driving the Tyrrell 006, powered by a Ford Cosworth engine numbered 066. François had seen it as a good omen, hoping to secure the first pole position of his career. He would have turned thirty just four months later, on February 25, 1974.

Cevert was Jackie Stewart's chosen successor at Tyrrell. Sadly, a fatal crash during qualifying at Watkins Glen in 1973 cut short his career and life.

FRANÇOIS CEVERT — *PARIS 02-25-1944*
WATKINS GLEN 10-06-1973

GP ENTERED	*46*
F1 WINS	*1*

CLAY REGAZZONI

Born in 1939, Gianclaudio Giuseppe Regazzoni worked in his family's auto body shop in Mendrisio when he started spending time with Silvio Moser, a fellow driver from the Italian-speaking Swiss canton of Ticino. Regazzoni entered racing relatively late, at twenty-four years old, in 1963. Today, that would be considered far too late to aspire to Formula 1, but back then, it wasn't unusual—especially since drivers often began their careers racing production cars. Regazzoni's rise was almost meteoric. In just a few years, he progressed from street cars to Formula 3 with Scuderia Martinelli and Sonvico, eventually earning a seat with Tecno in 1967.

By 1968, Clay had already started a family. After marrying Maria Pia, he became the father of their first child, Gianmaria, with their second, Alessia, arriving shortly thereafter. These responsibilities, however, had no impact on his conduct on the track. In Formula 3, the generous prize money motivated him to take more risks, and Clay certainly held his own among the many daredevils of the era. He was not only fast but also fearless in wheel-to-wheel battles, earning respect everywhere he raced. His career, however, was not without complications. In a terrifying Formula 3 crash at Monte Carlo, he miraculously emerged unscathed after sliding under the guardrail in his Tecno. Later, at Zandvoort, he was involved in an incident with British driver Chris Lambert, who tragically lost his life after going off-track during a Formula 2 race. In 1969, he was signed by Ferrari, but their Formula 2 program with Dino cars didn't last, and Regazzoni returned to Tecno. Nevertheless, the connection with Ferrari was firmly established.

In 1970, Ferrari focused on Jacky Ickx as their lead Formula 1 driver, with Clay sharing the second seat with Ignazio Giunti. After a solid debut, finishing fourth at the Dutch Grand Prix, the Swiss driver earned Enzo Ferrari's trust. In Austria, he finished second behind Ickx, and then came the big day at Monza. His triumph at the Italian Grand Prix in a Ferrari cemented his status shortly after turning thirty-one. Capping off a fantastic season, Regazzoni also won the European Formula 2 Championship with Tecno. The following two years were inconsistent, with highlights in the World Sportscar Championship but limited success in Formula 1. In 1973, Regazzoni joined BRM as Ferrari experienced one of the worst seasons in its history.

Recalled to Maranello, it was Regazzoni who recommended Niki Lauda, his teammate at BRM, to Ferrari. Clay was the quintessential driver of his era—a bon vivant, known for his jokes and his foot firmly on the gas, even on public roads. In 1974, Ferrari fielded a highly competitive car, but the rivalry between Clay and Lauda caused both to lose valuable points. Lauda claimed victories in Spain and the Netherlands, while Clay triumphed at

The Swiss driver, known for his iconic mustache, was left paralyzed after a crash in 1980.

CLAY REGAZZONI — *LUGANO 09-05-1939* / *FONTEVIVO 12-15-2006*

GP ENTERED	*132*
F1 WINS	*5*
POLE POSITIONS	*5*

the Nürburgring. Heading into the final race at Watkins Glen, the championship was a showdown between Regazzoni and Emerson Fittipaldi. However, Clay's title hopes were dashed early in the race when his Ferrari's front suspension mysteriously failed, leaving him with no chance of winning. The 1975 and 1976 Ferraris were formidable cars, but it was Niki Lauda—now fully in sync with the team—who capitalized, clinching the 1975 championship and narrowly missing out in 1976 after his infamous Nürburgring crash. Meanwhile, Regazzoni managed just two wins, at Monza in 1975 and Long Beach in 1976. By then, his relationship with Ferrari had soured, as evidenced by Enzo Ferrari's criticism that Clay was having "too much fun." After a couple of years with Ensign and Shadow, Regazzoni was signed by Williams to support Alan Jones. However, it was Clay who delivered Williams their first-ever Formula 1 victory, triumphing at Silverstone in 1979—a milestone for a team that would become legendary. Despite being over forty, he hadn't lost his passion for racing and returned to Ensign in 1980. At the United States Grand Prix in Long Beach, while running third, disaster struck. On the fastest straight, the titanium brake pedal shattered. With remarkable composure, Regazzoni sideswiped Zunino's Brabham, which was stationary in the short runoff area, before crashing head-on into a concrete wall. The impact with the Ensign was devastating. Emerson Fittipaldi, following closely behind, believed Clay had died instantly. However, he survived the crash, though severe spinal injuries left him a paraplegic for the rest of his life. Regazzoni embraced his new life with remarkable resilience and a deeper awareness of others'

Above: Niki Lauda (*in plain clothes*), Regazzoni, and Luca di Montezemolo review data after a practice session at the 1975 Swedish Grand Prix in Anderstorp.

Right: Regazzoni's Ferrari 312 T2 leads Alan Jones's Surtees out of the Noghes corner at Monte Carlo in 1976, the year Clay won at Long Beach.

13
durex
Marlboro
Ausonia
HEUER
GOODYEAR
Agip
2
Agip
GOODYEAR
Agip

suffering. Famous and admired, he inspired and supported many people with disabilities he met afterward. Using hand-controlled systems, he continued driving—and even racing—competing in the Paris-Dakar Rally and vintage car events. He also founded a driving school for people with disabilities and became a Formula 1 commentator for Italian television. However, his outspoken nature became more pronounced over the years, and his criticism of Mosley and Ecclestone following Ayrton Senna's fatal crash cost him his TV role. Despite this, Clay remained hugely popular and highly active, attending various events and initiatives supporting people with disabilities. On the evening of December 15, 2006, while driving his Chrysler Voyager to an event in Parma, he inexplicably crashed into a guardrail on the highway after colliding with a truck. He had a habit of not wearing a seat belt and died on impact. Strangely, for someone who was known to drive at full speed, he had been traveling at just 74.5 mph (120 km/h) in the right lane. Those who knew him believed he fell asleep at the wheel, as usual ignoring his fatigue, brought on by his frequent travels and still-busy lifestyle.

Above: 1977 F1 Championship. Regazzoni driving the Ensign, scoring points at the Argentine, Italian, and United States Grands Prix.

Right: Partnered with Alan Jones in 1979, Clay celebrated Williams's first of many Grand Prix victories at Silverstone.

Marlboro
Marlboro
ALBILAD
28
GOODYEAR

GOODYEAR
Borg-Warner
Marlboro
World Championship Team

EMERSON FITTIPALDI

Emerson Fittipaldi's father, Wilson, named him after the writer Ralph Waldo Emerson. Wilson was a motorsport enthusiast, commentator, and event organizer. At thirteen, Emerson began racing motorcycles but had to stop at sixteen when his parents found out. By then, he was already helping his older brother, Wilson Jr., as a kart mechanic. After giving up motorcycles, he followed in his brother's footsteps, becoming the Brazilian Karting Champion in 1963 and 1964. The Fittipaldi brothers eventually started building Formula Vee cars, and in 1967, Emerson won the national championship driving one of their creations. Using the money earned from selling the cars, he financed his racing career in Europe. In 1969, Emerson arrived in England and quickly made a name for himself in Formula Ford and Formula 3, where he won nine races and the MCD Lombard Championship.

He returned to England the following year with Maria Helena, his first wife, who was amazed at her husband's struggles with parking cars. By then, Emerson was already sporting his signature long sideburns, which became his hallmark and partially masked the scars left by his teenage acne. His protruding teeth earned him the nickname "Rato" (rat) among friends, while his brother, Wilson, with his imposing physique, was called "Tigrão" (big tiger). In 1970, Emerson started the season in Formula 2 with a semi-official Lotus, finishing every race in the top six, though without a win. Colin Chapman recognized his potential and gave him his Formula 1 debut at the British Grand Prix at Brands Hatch. Emerson's career skyrocketed after Jochen Rindt's tragic death at Monza in 1970. Suddenly, he was Lotus's lead driver. At the very next race, the United States Grand Prix at Watkins Glen—only the fifth Grand Prix of his career—Emerson secured a stunning victory, marking the start of his meteoric career. After a solid development season in 1971, which included a second-place finish in Austria, Fittipaldi dominated the 1972 championship behind the wheel of the Lotus 72. With five wins and three additional podiums, he became the youngest-ever World Champion at twenty-five. Emerson demonstrated exceptional maturity on the track, respecting the mechanics of his car and being fast without overdriving, showcasing superior tactical skills. Many considered him lucky, but much of his success stemmed from meticulous race preparation. In 1973, Colin Chapman signed Ronnie Peterson, regarded as the fastest driver of the era. While he started strong with back-to-back victories in Argentina, Brazil, and Spain, Jackie Stewart's resurgence and Peterson's three wins complicated his title defense. In 1974, Fittipaldi accepted an offer from McLaren in a season where the Ferraris of Regazzoni and Lauda were arguably the fastest cars on the grid. Emerson used all his tactical acumen to keep the title fight alive against Regazzoni until the final race at Watkins Glen. When the Swiss driver's Ferrari retired, it cleared the way for Emerson to claim his second World Championship. The following

After becoming a two-time Formula 1 World Champion, Fittipaldi repeated the feat at the Indianapolis 500.

EMERSON FITTIPALDI	SÃO PAULO 12-12-1946
GP ENTERED	144
F1 WINS	14
POLE POSITIONS	6
F1 WORLD CHAMPIONSHIPS	1972, 1974

The colors of the Lotus 72 and Fittipaldi's iconic helmet shine in a striking image from Clermont-Ferrand in 1972, the year of his first World Championship.

A pit stop for Fittipaldi's Penske Chevrolet during the 1989 Indianapolis 500, which the Brazilian driver won along with the CART Championship

in 1984, an IMSA race in Miami reignited his passion for competition. He was later offered the chance to race in the CART series, marking his return to the cockpit after four years away from racing. In 1989, at the age of forty-three, Emerson became the CART champion, driving a Penske for Patrick Racing and winning the Indianapolis 500 after a memorable final duel with Al Unser Jr. During this time, he had remarried Teresa, with whom he had two more children, Joana and Luca. His career in the United States continued with great success. In 1993, he won the Indianapolis 500 again, this time driving for the official Penske team. Nearly fifty years old, Emerson retired from professional racing at the end of 1996. Despite his age, he occasionally returned to the track: in 2005 in the Grand Prix Masters series, in 2008 in the Brazilian GT3 Championship, and in 2014, at the age of sixty-eight, competing in the 6 Hours of Interlagos in a Ferrari 458. After separating from Teresa, he had two more children, Emerson Jr. and Vittoria, with his last partner, Rossana. His legacy has been carried on by his grandson Pietro, Juliana's son, who has begun a successful racing career, proudly using his mother's last name and his grandfather Emerson's iconic helmet colors.

DAVID PURLEY

David Purley's career as a race car driver saw him win only the 1976 British Formula 5000 Championship. However, he is remembered not for his successes but for the immense courage he displayed on multiple occasions—most notably, his desperate attempt to save fellow driver Roger Williamson during the 1973 Dutch Grand Prix. Born in Bognor Regis on England's south coast just before the end of World War II, David was the son of the owner of a refrigerator company, LEC Refrigeration. As a young man, he learned to pilot airplanes before serving in the military as part of the Parachute Regiment in Aden. During the mid-1960s, he took part in operations against local insurgents and even survived a parachute jump where his chute partially failed to open. Displaying the cool headedness and bravery that would define him, David managed to survive the ordeal. Back in England, Purley began racing in 1968 with an AC Cobra, encouraged by his friendship with fellow local driver Derek Bell, who would later become one of the greatest sports car racers in history. After irreparably damaging the AC Cobra, Purley bought a 2-liter Chevron before stepping up to Formula 3 in 1970 with a Brabham sponsored by his family's company. He won his first race just weeks after his debut on the dangerous Chimay Street Circuit in Belgium, at the Grand Prix des Frontières. He beat none other than James Hunt and repeated the feat the following year, finishing ahead of Claude Bourgoignie, who had home advantage on the narrow streets of the Belgian city.

In 1972, Purley moved to Formula 2, driving a March, but returned to Chimay for the Formula 3 race, this time in an Ensign. In what was the last edition of the Grand Prix des Frontières, he won again, showing his fearless nature. Known for his proud and somewhat rebellious personality, Purley was also a very fast driver. Those close to him believed he didn't know fear, likely shaped by his experiences as a paratrooper. He started 1973 in Formula Atlantic but soon purchased a Formula 1 March. Competing under the colors of LEC Refrigeration, he entered several World Championship races, beginning with the Monaco Grand Prix. He skipped the British Grand Prix to race at Zandvoort in the Netherlands. During the competition, Purley was trailing fellow Brit Roger Williamson, a rising star driving a similar March. On the eighth lap, with cars still heavy with fuel, Williamson suffered a tire blowout and crashed into the barriers at over 124 mph (200 km/h). The March flipped, skidding for several feet before coming to a fiery stop. Purley didn't hesitate for a second. He pulled his car off the track and ran to help Williamson, who was trapped in the burning car. The live broadcast footage of the event was harrowing. Purley repeatedly tried to right Williamson's overturned March and then attempted to extinguish the flames alone, as the marshals, wearing civilian clothing that offered no fire protection, stood by helplessly. Despite his desperate efforts and repeated pleas for help from marshals and fellow drivers, Purley couldn't save Williamson and eventually collapsed, exhausted and devastated. The incident left a deep scar on Purley but did not lead him to retire from racing. For his heroic actions, he was awarded the George Medal by Queen Elizabeth II.

In 1974, Purley raced in Formula 2, finishing fifth in the European Championship. He returned to Formula 1 briefly, appearing in the British Grand Prix at Brands Hatch, but failed to qualify with the disastrous Token car he was given. Over the next two years, he competed in Formula 5000, driving heavy single-seaters and winning the 1976 British Championship in a Chevron. Purley's ambition remained to return to Formula 1, which he did in 1977 with a car he built himself under the LEC name. Although the car was far from competitive, Purley showed flashes of brilliance, such as at the Belgian Grand Prix at Zolder. In wet conditions, he stayed out on rain tires longer than his rivals, managing to hold off Niki Lauda's Ferrari for three laps before finishing three laps down from the winner, Gunnar Nilsson, in a Lotus.

At Silverstone, during pre-qualifying for the British Grand Prix, a stone jammed Purley's throttle wide open at the Copse corner. His LEC car crashed head-on into an embankment, experiencing an astonishing 180g deceleration as it went from 106 mph to zero in just 1.6 feet (170 km/h to zero in just half a meter). The wreck, with its chassis compressed to just over 3.3 feet (a meter), is now displayed at the Donington Park museum. Remarkably, Purley survived but sustained severe fractures to his legs and pelvis. After a lengthy rehabilitation, he returned to racing in 1979, competing in the Aurora Formula 1 Championship with a Shadow, finishing fourth at Snetterton. He participated in a few minor races before retiring from cars and taking up aerobatic flying. Purley's need for speed and control at the edge of a vehicle's capabilities found expression in his Pitts Special biplane. On July 2, 1985, while performing aerobatics a mile off the coast of his home in Bognor Regis, Purley failed to pull out of a dive and crashed into the sea, dying instantly.

A man of immense courage and determination, David Purley is remembered for his heroic attempt to save Williamson from the flames at the 1973 Dutch Grand Prix.

DAVID PURLEY *BOGNOR REGIS 01-26-1945*
BOGNOR REGIS 07-02-1985

GP ENTERED *7*

MARIO ANDRETTI

In 1954, at just fourteen years old, Mario Gabriele Andretti was in Monza, admiring his idol, Alberto Ascari. He undoubtedly dreamed of becoming a driver, but it's unlikely he could have imagined what would happen to him in the years to come. His family was originally from Montona, on the Istrian Peninsula, which was Italian when Mario and his twin brother, Aldo, were born. After the war, in 1948, the Andretti family was displaced to Lucca, waiting to immigrate elsewhere after Istria was annexed by the newly formed Yugoslavia. In 1955, they arrived in Nazareth, Pennsylvania, to begin a new life. Mario and Aldo, already infected by the racing bug, worked in a garage and bought an old Hudson, which they began racing on the dirt track in town. They were fast, usually either winning or crashing out. Aldo suffered a serious accident, fracturing his skull, which effectively ended his racing career. Their parents found out and were furious, but Mario was unstoppable—especially as he kept winning race after race. At twenty-one, he was a star in Midget racing, competing in single-seaters still raced on dirt ovals today. In 1964, he debuted in the USAC, America's premier category, driving Formula Indy cars.

In Nazareth, Mario met the lovely Dee Ann Hoch, two years younger than him, who helped him improve his English. They married in 1961, starting a union that would last despite the inevitable temptations of a driver's lifestyle. Mario wisely avoided competing in the Indianapolis 500 in his first year. In 1965, he entered the race for the first time, finishing third and earning the "Rookie of the Year" award. By the end of the year, he won the championship—the first of an uninterrupted streak of titles until 1969. That season, he finally won the Indianapolis 500, an achievement that, surprisingly, would remain the only one in his incredibly long career. During those years, Mario didn't limit himself to Formula Indy cars. He raced in Can-Am with Lola and at Le Mans with Ford and even won the legendary Daytona 500 in 1967, reserved for stock cars. In 1968, Lotus signed him for the Italian Grand Prix at Monza, on the same weekend as the Hoosier 100 in the United States. Mario and Al Unser, racing for BRM, planned an audacious schedule: qualify at Monza on Friday, race in the US on Saturday, and return for Sunday's Grand Prix. Both were stopped by Monza officials, citing safety concerns. At Watkins Glen during the United States Grand Prix, Mario returned to the Lotus 49, setting a sensational pole position before retiring from the race. His Formula 1 experience continued with three races in 1969, but without notable results.

In 1970, Andretti became the "hero of two worlds," racing in

In the United States, Andretti fulfilled his dream of becoming a racing driver—a dream he had begun nurturing in Italy while following Ascari's exploits.

MARIO ANDRETTI *MONTONA 02-28-1940*

GP ENTERED	*128*
F1 WINS	*12*
POLE POSITIONS	*18*
F1 WORLD CHAMPIONSHIPS	*1978*

In 1979, Andretti also used the Simpson Bandit helmet, which was briefly popular among drivers, not only in Formula 1. Here he is pictured on the Lotus at Hockenheim.

the United States and in Formula 1 with March, while also competing in the World Sportscar Championship with Ferrari. He won at Sebring and Watkins Glen with the Ferrari 512 S. In 1971, he joined the Maranello team for select Grands Prix alongside Jacky Ickx and Clay Regazzoni, winning the season-opening South African Grand Prix at Kyalami and a non-championship race in Ontario, California. However, further success eluded him, and he had to settle for the 1972 World Sportscar title. Andretti returned to the US full-time in 1973 and 1974 before reappearing in Formula 1 with the underwhelming Parnelli Jones team. Meanwhile, Colin Chapman's Lotus team, struggling with technical issues, asked Mario to return.

Andretti's vast experience across various cars had made him an exceptional test driver, adept at identifying tweaks to enhance performance. His victories with Ferrari, particularly at Sebring with the massive 5-liter prototype, earned him the nickname "Piedone" (big foot) in Italy. In 1976, after steady improvement, Lotus returned to victory at the rain-soaked Japanese Grand Prix, remembered for Niki Lauda's decision to withdraw due to the perilous conditions. Once again, Lotus surprised everyone with a revolutionary innovation: ground-effect aerodynamics. Andretti skillfully exploited this new advantage. Despite four wins to Lauda's three in 1977, Andretti lost the championship due to the unreliable Lotus 78. However, in 1978,

Andretti at the wheel of the Lotus 78 Ford V8 during the Monaco Grand Prix on May 7, 1978. The British team dominated the championship that year.

he and teammate Ronnie Peterson dominated the season. The tragic loss of Peterson at Monza cast a shadow over what was otherwise a triumphant season. Andretti's final two years with Lotus marked a decline for both the team and the driver. In 1981, he made an unsuccessful attempt to revive Alfa Romeo in Formula 1. The following year, he returned to Ferrari for the Italian Grand Prix at Monza, earning a fantastic pole position and finishing third in front of a crowd that still adored him.

Having definitively left Europe and Formula 1—becoming the most frequent passenger on the Concorde—Mario continued racing in the United States, winning the CART Championship in 1984 before officially retiring in 1994. He also made a final attempt at the 24 Hours of Le Mans, a race he never won, and an incredible return to the Indianapolis 500 in 1993 at age sixty-three, which ended with a terrifying crash during practice. Always kind and beloved by everyone, not just journalists, Andretti has maintained ties with his homeland, continuing to speak Italian with fellow Italians, even as a proud American citizen since 1964. He has three children. His two sons, Michael and Jeff, pursued racing careers with considerable success. Today, Mario is a wealthy gentleman involved in numerous business ventures, including Andretti Autosport, founded by Michael. On the track, it's now his cherished grandson Marco, Michael's son, who carries on the family's legacy.

RONNIE PETERSON

Ronnie Peterson made a name for himself in Formula 3, competing across Europe after leaving his native Sweden. He raced wherever he could, drawn by the lucrative prizes offered to attract the best drivers in the category. Born in Örebro, in the heart of Scandinavia, Peterson was naturally shy and introverted. However, once behind the wheel, he transformed into an unstoppable force. Like Jochen Rindt, he loved sliding the car sideways, pushing the limits of grip with counter-steering. He wasn't just incredibly fast but also strikingly handsome. Tall, blond, and good looking, he had a beautiful girlfriend, Barbro, who followed him almost everywhere.

After seven years between karting and Formula 3, Peterson found himself on Formula 1 grids in 1970, alongside the world's best drivers. His privately entered March wasn't very competitive, but Ronnie still managed to shine, building a reputation as a courageous and consistently fast driver. As he grew comfortable with the more powerful single-seaters, Peterson began racking up significant finishes in 1971. By the season's end, he was second in the championship standings, behind Jackie Stewart, who claimed his second title that year. March was a team with limited resources. After producing a strong car in 1971, they provided Peterson and his teammate Niki Lauda with an uncompetitive and difficult car in 1972. Consolation came with his Ferrari contract to race the 312 PB in the World Sportscar Championship, which Ferrari won decisively, with Peterson contributing significantly.

By then, Peterson was ready for a top team, and it was no surprise when he joined Lotus in 1973 alongside reigning World Champion Emerson Fittipaldi. Ronnie had to wait until July for his first Formula 1 win at the French Grand Prix, starting a series of victories that, nonetheless, couldn't stop Stewart from clinching another world title. Peterson's career seemed poised for a championship run as he became the Lotus team leader in 1974, even partnered with a driver like Jacky Ickx. Unfortunately, the team completely botched the design of the new Lotus 74, forcing Peterson to rely on a heavily modified Lotus 72, which had debuted four years earlier with Rindt. Despite this, Peterson made the car fly, achieving nearly impossible victories at Monaco, Dijon, and Monza. Always driving on the edge, he could extract the maximum potential from any car he was given. However, his weakness lay in car development—he was a poor tester and unable to suggest the changes needed to improve the car's handling.

Instead, he adapted to the car's flaws, which, combined with his aggressive style, strained the mechanical components, leading to more retirements than average. After another disappointing season with Lotus, Peterson returned to March in 1976, where he pulled off another miraculous win at Monza. The following year, he was rumored to be heading to Ferrari, but Maranello chose Villeneuve, leaving Peterson with the heavy and complex six-wheeled Tyrrell for another difficult season. At home, he found solace in spending hours watching the fish in his aquarium, though he may not have been as calm as he appeared. Barbro, now his wife, confided to some journalists that Ronnie often struggled to sleep in the days leading up to Grands Prix. The couple, who had welcomed their first daughter, Nina Louise, had settled in Monte Carlo.

Meanwhile, Lotus had risen again under Mario Andretti's leadership, thanks to his development skills and the revolutionary discovery of ground-effect aerodynamics. Colin Chapman brought Peterson back in 1978 under a strict second-driver contract. Mechanics were instructed to add extra fuel to his car during qualifying to give Andretti an advantage. In races, Peterson was often faster than his teammate but as a fair, consummate professional never challenged him and settled for following Andretti across the finish line. He still managed to win in South Africa with the Lotus 78 and in Austria with the Lotus 79, during a season he and Andretti dominated.

Then came the weekend of the Italian Grand Prix at Monza, one of the rare occasions Barbro stayed home in Monte Carlo with Nina. During the morning practice session, Peterson destroyed his sturdier Lotus 79 and had to start the race with the older, more fragile 78. After a poor start, he was caught between Reutemann's Ferrari and Hunt's McLaren just a few hundred feet after the green flag. In the chaos, Peterson crashed nearly head-on into the guardrail, and the Lotus caught fire, which was fortunately extinguished quickly. Peterson suffered fractured legs, one of which was severely injured, but his life was not in danger. At Niguarda Hospital, doctors decided to operate to reduce the fractures. Complications arose after surgery, and an unexpected fat embolism claimed Ronnie Peterson's life, leaving fans and the racing world in disbelief. For Barbro, the loss was unbearable; in 1987, she took her own life, unable to cope without him. Their daughter, Nina Louise, has since become a mother to two children, one of whom is named Max Ronnie.

Many consider Ronnie Peterson the fastest driver of the 1970s. His Achilles' heel was car development.

RONNIE PETERSON *ÖREBRO 02-14-1944*
MILAN 09-11-1978

GP ENTERED	*123*
F1 WINS	*10*
POLE POSITIONS	*14*

JODY SCHECKTER

In East London, where Jody Scheckter was born, his father owned a Renault dealership. This made it easy for Jody to get involved with motorcycles and cars from a very young age. By the time he was eighteen, he was already one of the fastest drivers in the South African touring car championship, racing a Renault tuned in his family garage. As a driver, Scheckter was far from calm. In his debut season, he managed to get disqualified for dangerous driving before racking up a string of victories. After completing his military service, he joined the national Formula Ford Championship in 1970, winning it and earning the "Driver for Europe" award. This came with prize money and round-trip tickets to England. Just over twenty years old, Jody moved to Europe with his wife, Pamela, whom he called Pam.

In the UK, Scheckter quickly made a name for himself. His driving was aggressive—some even called it wild—and his untamed curly hair framed by enormous sideburns contributed to his image as a rough-around-the-edges young driver. At his Formula Ford debut at Brands Hatch, driving a Merlyn, he stunned the crowd by leading the pack before spinning out. He soon began winning but often pushed too hard, spinning out as he tested both his own and the car's limits. Mid-season, he moved up to Formula 3, where he started winning more consistently and making fewer mistakes, earning a Formula 2 seat with McLaren. Although the season wasn't particularly successful, Scheckter won a race at Crystal Palace, prompting McLaren to reward him. By the end of the year—just eighteen months after arriving in England—he was behind the wheel of a Formula 1 car at the United States Grand Prix at Watkins Glen. Qualifying eighth, he finished ninth and secured a position as McLaren's third driver for several races in 1973, alongside Peter Revson and Denny Hulme. His second race of the season, at the French Grand Prix at Le Castellet, made waves. Starting on the front row alongside Emerson Fittipaldi, Scheckter led the race for over forty laps before an impatient Fittipaldi attempted a difficult overtake, colliding with the McLaren and ending the race for both drivers. Suddenly, everyone was talking about Jody, especially Fittipaldi, who accused him of being a danger to others. Scheckter became even more infamous just two weeks later at the British Grand Prix at Silverstone. Pushing to the limit, he attempted to take Woodcote corner in fourth gear during the race—a maneuver possible only with an empty fuel tank during qualifying. The result was a spectacular 360-degree spin, leaving his McLaren stationary in the middle of the track. The ensuing pileup involved fifteen cars, making it one of the most massive crashes in Formula 1 history. Fortunately, no one was seriously injured, although de Adamich suffered a fractured ankle. Scheckter's appearance and demeanor didn't endear him to his peers.

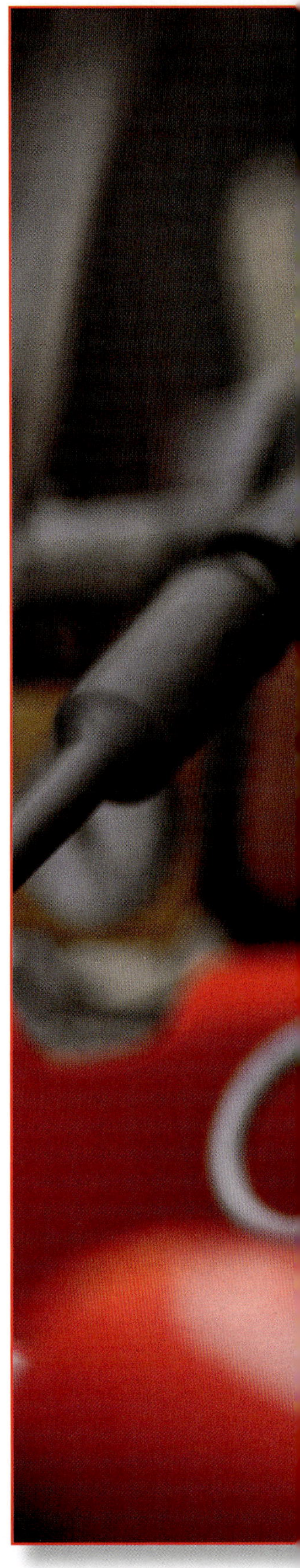

From a reckless, risk-taking driver, Jody Scheckter transformed into a careful champion after witnessing François Cevert's fatal crash.

Left: Joining Ferrari in 1979, Scheckter fully capitalized on the potential of the 312 T4, winning the World Championship. Here he is pictured at Monte Carlo, ahead of Villeneuve.

Above: Gilles Villeneuve and Jody Scheckter formed a close partnership. The Canadian always respected his teammate, and the feeling was mutual.

He spoke little but was direct and blunt when he did. He wasn't exactly considered a gentleman, even by those who observed him struggling with cutlery at restaurants. Instead of mingling with powerful figures who attended races, he preferred spending time with mechanics. After being temporarily sidelined by McLaren, Scheckter raced in Canada, where he collided with François Cevert, further fueling criticism of the South African. By a twist of fate, two weeks later, Jody was the first driver to arrive at the scene of Cevert's fatal crash. The incident deeply affected him, leading him to change his driving style. Tyrrell then signed Scheckter, having decided to invest in him even before Jackie Stewart announced his retirement. Under Tyrrell's mentorship—Scheckter affectionately called him "Uncle Ken"—and with Stewart's guidance, he transformed into a more composed and reliable driver. He delivered an impressive series of results, including victories at the Swedish and British Grand Prix in 1974. The following year, he won his home race at Kyalami and drove the experimental six-wheeled Tyrrell in 1976. Although innovative in its aerodynamic concepts, the car was too heavy to dominate. Nevertheless, Scheckter won again at the Swedish Grand Prix. In 1977, he took on the challenge of debuting the Wolf team, sensationally winning the season opener in Argentina and following it up with wins at Monaco and Canada, finishing third in the World Championship.

After a disappointing 1978 season, Scheckter joined Ferrari, partnered with Gilles Villeneuve. The Canadian's speed and determination were remarkable, but the now-mature Scheckter maximized the superior 312 T4 and Michelin tires with consistent podium finishes and wins at Zolder, Monza, and Montreal, while Villeneuve was often forced to retire. The two drivers were great friends and worked well together. At Monza, on the day Scheckter secured his World Championship title, Villeneuve followed closely behind but didn't challenge him, even though he could have. Having won the title, Scheckter was given a very uncompetitive Ferrari in 1980 and seemed to have given all he had to Formula 1. He retired at the end of the season, not yet thirty-one years old. Scheckter later separated from Pam, with whom he had two sons, Tomas and Toby, both of whom became racers. He moved to the United States and proved to be a skilled entrepreneur, founding a company specializing in personal defense training simulations. To everyone's surprise, he returned to England and established Laverstoke Park Farm, a biodynamic and organic farm producing meat and cheeses, including mozzarella, with great success. Scheckter remarried Clare, with whom he has four more children.

JODY SCHECKTER	*EAST LONDON 01-29-1950*
GP ENTERED	*110*
F1 WINS	*10*
POLE POSITIONS	*3*
F1 WORLD CHAMPIONSHIPS	*1979*

NIKI LAUDA

His full name was Andreas Nikolaus Lauda, but to everyone, he was simply Niki. The three-time Formula 1 World Champion began his career against the wishes of his family, wealthy Austrian industrialists. Even as a young man, he showed a knack for raising funds to purchase his first cars, including a Mini that he debuted in a hill climb race in 1968. When his father found out, he forbade him from racing, but nothing could quell Niki's passion. He soon moved from the Mini to a Porsche 911 and, the following year, to Formula Vee, winning a couple of races. Once in Formula 3 in 1970, his results were unremarkable, though he found consolation in a couple of first-place finishes in a Porsche 908.

In 1971, thanks to his family's prominent name, he secured a loan from a bank to race in Formula 2 with the March team. In the following season, as he prepared to debut in Formula 1 with March, he sought another loan from the same bank, but his father intervened to block it. Niki severed ties with his family and managed to secure funding from another bank. Unfortunately, the 1972 March Formula 1 car was a disappointment, and the expected results did not materialize. By the end of the year, Niki was in despair. Instead of giving up, he secured another loan to race with BRM in 1973. A few strong performances, including a sixth-place finish at Monaco, drew attention and brought in sponsorship from BMW for touring car races, helping him pay off his debts. Among his teammates at BRM was Clay Regazzoni, who was returning to Ferrari and recommended Lauda to the Maranello team. Once with Ferrari, Lauda embarked on an intense testing and development program, fully utilizing the Fiorano test track. He had been engaged for four years to Mariella Reininghaus, an elegant woman from Salzburg whose family owned a well-known mineral water and beverage brand. While he may not have been the outright fastest driver, his determination and relentless drive to improve the car were unmatched. Ferrari nicknamed him "the computer," which perfectly encapsulated his methodical approach to racing.

In 1974, Lauda secured his first wins in Spain and the Netherlands. However, a crash at the Nürburgring and a series of retirements took him out of contention for the title, which went to Emerson Fittipaldi, with Regazzoni finishing second. Ferrari was back at the top, and in 1975 the 312 T proved almost unbeatable. Niki's hard work paid off with five victories, earning him his first World Championship. Meanwhile, after irreconcilable differences with Mariella, he married the stunning Marlene Knaus, who would later become the mother of their sons, Mathias and Lukas.

Niki Lauda in the cockpit of the Ferrari 312 T, the formidable car in which he won his first World Championship

NIKI LAUDA	VIENNA 02-22-1949 ZURICH 05-20-2019
GP ENTERED	171
F1 WINS	25
POLE POSITIONS	24
F1 WORLD CHAMPIONSHIPS	1975, 1977, 1984

Nürburgring, 1976: Lauda in the cockpit as Tomaini, Audetto, and Regazzoni speak with him. During the race, he suffered the most terrible accident of his career.

In 1976, despite strong competition from James Hunt's McLaren, Lauda seemed poised to defend his title. Then came the infamous Nürburgring crash. On the second lap, his Ferrari spun out near Bergwerk, hitting an embankment and bursting into flames in the middle of the track. Trapped in the cockpit without a helmet—it blew off during the impact—Lauda was rescued by Arturo Merzario, Harald Ertl, Brett Lunger, and Guy Edwards. Taken to Mannheim Hospital, he was in critical condition due to inhaling toxic fumes but ultimately survived, though he suffered severe burns to his face and ears that left permanent scars. Ferrari skipped the Austrian Grand Prix, returning in the Netherlands with Regazzoni as the sole driver. By the Italian Grand Prix at Monza, Ferrari had signed Carlos Reutemann as Lauda's replacement. However, astonishingly, Niki returned to the grid just six weeks after his accident. Ferrari entered three cars, with Lauda finishing fourth, reigniting his championship hopes. His battle with James Hunt, immortalized in Ron Howard's film *Rush*, culminated at the rain-soaked Japanese Grand Prix. Deeming the conditions too dangerous, Lauda withdrew after the first lap, and Hunt clinched the title by finishing third.

After retiring in 1979, the Austrian returned to racing with McLaren in 1982, winning at Long Beach and Silverstone (*pictured*).

By 1977, Lauda's relationship with Ferrari had deteriorated. By focusing on consistency, Niki was crowned World Champion despite Mario Andretti scoring more victories. In 1978, amid much controversy, Lauda moved to Brabham, where he won the Swedish Grand Prix with a "fan car" (immediately banned) and the Italian Grand Prix after penalties to Andretti and Gilles Villeneuve. In mid-1979, he abruptly retired to focus on his passion for aviation. After earning his pilot's license, he founded Lauda Air, but financial struggles led to his sensational return to Formula 1 with McLaren in 1982. He won at Long Beach and Silverstone that year. Two years later, powered by Porsche engines, McLaren became the team to beat. However, Lauda now had an uncomfortable teammate in Alain Prost. As always, Niki focused on race preparation rather than being fazed by Prost's qualifying times. His strategy paid off, earning him a third World Championship by just half a point over Prost. In 1985, Lauda retired for good at the end of the season.

After retiring, Lauda began a long entrepreneurial career with ups and downs. He served as an advisor to Ferrari from 1993 to 1995, sold Lauda Air to Austrian Airlines in 1999, and

Left: The Austrian driver with McLaren in 1985, where he had the satisfaction of beating Alain Prost at the Dutch Grand Prix in Zandvoort

founded FlyNiki, a low-cost airline. He returned to Formula 1 as Jaguar's Team Principal in 2001 and 2002 before becoming a television commentator. In 2012, Mercedes hired him as a non-executive chairman of their Formula 1 team, where he played a key role in convincing Lewis Hamilton to leave McLaren—a decision that yielded legendary results. Lauda's personal life was equally eventful. In 2008, he married Birgit Wetzinger, a flight attendant who donated a kidney to him. They had two children together. Lauda had received his first kidney transplant in 1997, donated by his brother, likely due to complications from the Nürburgring crash. Unfortunately, his health declined in his later years. In 2018, he underwent a lung transplant following a severe infection and never fully recovered. After being on dialysis for a prolonged period, he passed away on May 20, 2019.

Right: Niki Lauda during the Austrian Grand Prix at Zeltweg in 1984, a race he won, earning crucial championship points

TEXACO
GOODYEAR
Marlboro
James Hunt
A Rh +

JAMES HUNT

The second of six children in a large Surrey family, James Simon Wallis Hunt was the son of a stockbroker. From an early age, he displayed a strong and willful personality, excelling in sports like cricket, tennis, squash, and golf. He became passionate about racing after getting his driver's license and visiting Silverstone on his eighteenth birthday. While working various odd jobs, he saved up to buy a Mini, which he raced, though he was disqualified in his first start due to a seat irregularity. By 1969, he was competing in Formula Ford, renting a car and earning his first wins. Hunt began making a name for himself in 1970, not just for his victories in Formula 3, such as at Rouen and Zolder in a Lotus, but also for numerous crashes and a post-race scuffle with Dave Morgan that nearly turned into a fistfight. The British press and fans nicknamed him "Hunt the Shunt," but his undeniable skills behind the wheel couldn't be overlooked. In 1972, he joined March as an official Formula 3 driver but was dropped mid-season after publicly criticizing the car, calling it "a piece of junk." His turbulent reputation and inconsistent results threatened to derail his career. A stroke of luck came when he met Alexander Hesketh, a young aristocrat smitten with racing and eager to spend his wealth having fun. Perhaps drawn by James's carefree attitude and striking looks, Lord Hesketh bankrolled a Formula 2 team, using a March car for his driver. A third-place finish at Oulton Park convinced Hesketh of Hunt's talent. Since Formula 1 costs weren't much higher, the team entered the 1973 season, again with a March single-seater. Hunt repaid the faith with a third-place finish in the Netherlands and a second-place result in the US, where he also set the fastest lap.

Thrilled with his driver's performance, Lord Hesketh decided to develop an in-house car, designed by Harvey Postlethwaite, who would later gain fame with Tyrrell and Ferrari. Hunt forged a close friendship with the team's sporting director, Anthony "Bubbles" Horsley, a fellow bon vivant. At over six feet tall, with enormous size-fourteen feet that required cutting the toes off his racing boots to maintain circulation, Hunt stood out as much for his blond, handsome looks as for his speed. His jumpsuit bore a patch reading "Sex: Breakfast of Champions," leaving little to the imagination. Despite his devil-may-care attitude, Hunt wasn't fearless. Fully aware of the dangers of racing, he sometimes vomited before events, whether from nerves or the excesses of the night before. A heavy smoker—up to forty cigarettes a day—and a fan of drinking to excess, he found himself perfectly at home in the Hesketh team. Known

James Hunt, 1976 Formula 1 World Champion, was a unique figure in the history of motorsport.

JAMES HUNT — *LONDON 08-29-1947* / *WIMBLEDON 06-15-1993*

GP ENTERED	*92*
F1 WINS	*10*
POLE POSITIONS	*14*
F1 WORLD CHAMPIONSHIPS	*1976*

Hunt in action with the McLaren M23, the car that earned him the 1976 World Championship after a third-place finish in the season's final race in Japan

For consuming more champagne and lobster than fuel, their parties were legendary, complete with Rolls-Royces, helicopters, and an endless parade of beautiful women. In 1974, Hunt claimed his first non-championship victory at Silverstone and racked up three podiums over the season. In 1975, he earned his first Grand Prix win at Zandvoort. The race started on a wet track, and Hunt capitalized on a tire change to take the lead. Though Ferrari's Niki Lauda chased him down, Hunt held his nerve under immense pressure. That year was personally tumultuous, marked by the collapse of his marriage to the stunning model Suzy Miller. James, ill-suited for domestic life, wasn't fazed when she left him for the older actor Richard Burton, who covered their divorce costs. The split only gave Hunt more freedom to indulge in his hedonistic lifestyle, often alongside motorcycle champion Barry Sheene, his close friend and partner in mischief.

In 1976, McLaren signed Hunt to replace Emerson Fittipaldi, despite concerns about his lifestyle. Fast as ever, Hunt delivered in a season marked by drama and controversy. He won in Spain, though the victory was temporarily annulled, and he was disqualified at Brands Hatch for using a spare car. The horrific accident of his friend Niki Lauda shook Hunt

The podium of the 1976 British Grand Prix: Hunt celebrates, though he was later disqualified for using a spare car after the first start.

though Lauda's misfortune reopened the championship fight. Contrary to depictions in recent films, the two were, in fact, genuine friends. Hunt clinched the title with a hard-fought third-place finish at the final race in Japan. The following year, Hunt seemed affected by his newfound fame and excesses. He still managed victories at Silverstone, Watkins Glen, and Fuji, but his final win came under contentious circumstances: He skipped the podium, citing a tight schedule. His 1978 season yielded just one third-place finish in France, and the death of his friend Ronnie Peterson at the Italian Grand Prix deeply affected him. Joining Wolf Racing in 1979, Hunt retired mid-season, citing poor results and the ever-present dangers of racing. At just thirty-one, he walked away from Formula 1. The BBC hired him as a Grand Prix commentator, a role he embraced with sharp, often-cutting observations. He moved to Wimbledon, where he raised parrots and remarried in 1982, fathering two sons, Peter and David. True to form—he was a compulsive cheater—Hunt separated from his second wife, Sarah Lomax, before beginning a relationship with Helen Dyson, eighteen years his junior. On June 15, 1993, mere hours after proposing to Dyson, Hunt suffered a fatal heart attack at his Wimbledon home. He was just forty-five.

GILLES VILLENEUVE

Even though he only won six Grands Prix and his career at the top lasted less than four years, Gilles Villeneuve left an indelible mark on Formula 1 history. Few drivers have stirred such passion and debate as this short Canadian, born in January 1950 in Saint-Jean-sur-Richelieu. Gilles, however, always claimed to be born in 1952 to align better with the timeline of a Grand Prix driver. Raised in Berthierville, he quickly fell in love with driving and engines alongside his younger brother, Jacques. By sixteen, he had his driver's license, he was married to Joanna by twenty, and a year later he became a father to Jacques, soon followed by Mélanie. Gilles began racing on dangerous snowmobiles, which demanded not only courage but also a good dose of recklessness. He excelled, reaching speeds of 87 mph (140 km/h) in elbow-to-elbow battles with relentless competitors, using his winnings to fund summer car races. By 1973, he had already claimed the Quebec Formula Ford title. At the start of 1974, he became the world snowmobile champion by clinching the title in Eagle River, Wisconsin. Passionate about mechanics, Gilles loved dismantling and reassembling anything—even electrical appliances—just to understand how they worked. His snowmobile featured a custom rear suspension he designed, which proved successful in races. With his snow racing earnings, he made his debut in Formula Atlantic, navigating incredible financial difficulties until Montreal magnate Gilles Parent spotted his talent in 1976 after he battled Keke Rosberg and won his first wet race in Gimli. Driving a March, Gilles won nine out of ten races, securing the championship title. At Trois-Rivières, he left behind Hunt, Brambilla, Jones, Tambay, and Depailler—Formula 1 drivers who were entered in the season's marquee race. Hunt spoke highly of him to McLaren's Teddy Mayer. Still racing (and winning) in Formula Atlantic in 1977, Gilles suddenly got a call to drive for McLaren at the British Grand Prix at Silverstone. Though the car was outdated, the Canadian still impressed: He was running seventh when a faulty thermometer reading caused him to pit unnecessarily. When Ferrari needed to replace Lauda—who left abruptly after reclaiming the championship—Villeneuve got the call. When contacted in Canada, Gilles initially thought it was a prank. Enzo Ferrari, however, loved taking chances and wanted to prove he could win with an unknown Canadian. Gilles made his debut with Ferrari in Montreal in 1977, but it wasn't a standout performance.

Choosing Villeneuve was a gamble for Enzo Ferrari. After a rough start in Formula 1, the Canadian became one of the sport's most beloved drivers.

GILLES VILLENEUVE — *SAINT-JEAN-SUR-RICHELIEU 01-18-1950*
LOVANIO 05-08-1982

GP ENTERED	*67*
F1 WINS	*6*
POLE POSITIONS	*2*

Villeneuve, leading at the start of the 1979 Austrian Grand Prix. He was often faster than his teammate Scheckter, who went on to win the World Championship.

At Fuji in Japan, a misstep by Peterson caused Gilles's Ferrari to launch over the Swede's Lotus, tragically striking two spectators who shouldn't have been there. Both lost their lives, and criticism quickly followed. At the end of the year, Gilles moved his family to Cannes so his children could attend school in their mother tongue. Villeneuve gave everything on the track, fearless and always pushing to 100 percent. 1978 began on a rough note. He was leading at Long Beach when he soared over Regazzoni's lapped Shadow, earning him the nickname "the Aviator." Then, in Monaco, he had a terrifying crash exiting the tunnel due to a tire blowout. Ferrari defended him against critics, giving him time to mature, and by the end of the year, Gilles claimed his first victory in Montreal. In 1979, he was often faster than his teammate Scheckter, winning in South Africa and twice in the United States at Long Beach and Watkins Glen. Gilles delivered spectacular performances but often retired while Scheckter collected crucial points and three victories to become World Champion. Fans were electrified by his feats, like the wheel-to-wheel duel with Arnoux in France or his three-wheeled return to the pits in the Netherlands, showcasing unmatched tenacity. His driving style was breathtaking and unrelenting, always chasing opponents or the fastest lap. Off the track, Gilles drove just as wildly, speeding

In 1981, Gilles achieved two unlikely victories, in Monaco and Spain, with Ferrari's first turbo car, the 126 CK.

everywhere, convinced of his absolute car control—so much so that he didn't adjust his style even with his children on board.

Ferrari struggled in 1980, but in 1981 they gave Gilles his first turbocharged car. It was a handful to drive, but he pulled off miracles, winning in Monaco and Spain by holding off Laffite, Watson, Reutemann, and de Angelis for the entire race. His teammate Didier Pironi became a close friend on and off the track. Meanwhile, Gilles earned his helicopter pilot's license in just three weeks, treating himself to a seven-seater Agusta A109. He used it to travel across Europe, often flying low to read highway signs. Among his "toys" was also a powerful offshore speedboat, as he continued to live with the spirit of a young boy. Finally, in 1982, Ferrari seemed to have a car—the 126 C2—capable of securing the title. However, his relationship with Pironi soured at Imola. Despite a team order to slow down, Pironi overtook Villeneuve in the final moments of the race. Gilles felt robbed and betrayed, especially after respecting Scheckter three years earlier. Just two weeks later, during qualifying at Zolder for the Belgian Grand Prix, Gilles tried to beat Pironi's time but tragically collided with Jochen Mass's March. His Ferrari launched into the air, and Gilles was thrown out, dying almost instantly.

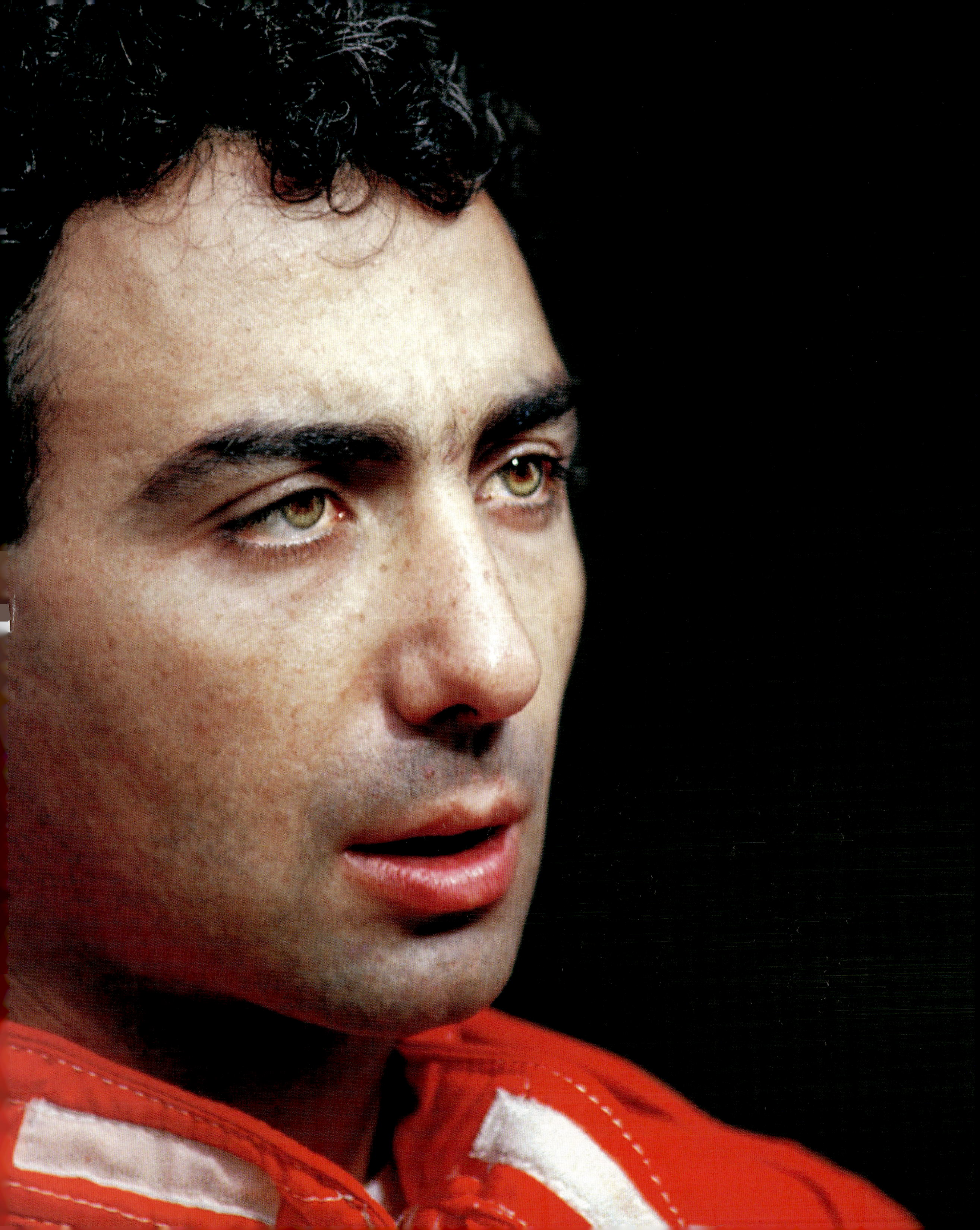

MICHELE ALBORETO

Until the age of eighteen, Michele Alboreto was just another young guy with a passion for racing, spending time at the Monza racetrack whenever he had the chance. Growing up in Milan's suburbs, he was one of the few to pull off the near miracle of reaching the top levels of motorsport after starting from almost nothing. After earning his driver's license, he had to save up for a used Formula Monza car with a bent chassis. But even then, those who knew racing could already see his talent. Under the wing of Scuderia Salvati, he advanced to Formula Italia and then Formula 3 in 1979, thanks to loans from supporters who believed in him. He immediately stood out as one of the most promising in the category, landing a spot with one of Italy's top teams. His first major victory came in 1980, when he won the European Formula 3 Championship while driving a March for Team Euroracing after a season-long duel with his fiercest rival, Thierry Boutsen.

Michele knew the road ahead was still steep. His determined personality and unshakable willpower as well as the support of friends and sponsors had already taken him far, but he needed more. In 1981, he hoped to secure a seat with an official Formula 2 team but found himself without a ride. Giancarlo Minardi—a passionate figure who would later establish the eponymous Formula 1 team—came to the rescue. The Minardi car was no match for the Marches, Ralts, or Spirits of the top teams, but Alboreto embraced the challenge. Then, suddenly, a breakthrough: With the backing of Italian patron Count Gughi Zanon, he got the call from Tyrrell to race in the San Marino Grand Prix at Imola. Running in the points, a collision with Beppe Gabbiani's Osella cut his debut short. Still, the opportunity confirmed his place in Formula 1. At Misano, later that season, he even managed a win for Minardi in a European Formula 2 race.

Michele was almost always accompanied at races by his girlfriend, Nadia, whom he'd met as a teenager in Rozzano. Alboreto was a die-hard Ronnie Peterson fan, and his helmet sported the Swedish legend's blue-and-yellow colors. Michele described himself as an attacking driver—gritty and unwilling to give up. When things didn't go his way (which happened often), he channeled his anger into determination and the drive to win. Respected by all, especially on the track, he pushed forward with a desperate need to seize every opportunity. Under the guidance of Ken Tyrrell, a master at spotting talent, Michele grew significantly as both a driver and a person. In 1982, he scored his first Formula 1 victory in Las Vegas, capping a season where he was consistently near the top. He followed it up with another win the next year in Detroit, at the other United States Grand Prix. By then, it was clear Michele was ready for

Years after Ascari, Michele Alboreto was the only Italian driver to come close to winning the World Championship with Ferrari.

MICHELE ALBORETO *MILAN 12-23-1956*
KLETTWITZ 04-25-2001

GP ENTERED	*194*
F1 WINS	*5*
POLE POSITIONS	*2*

Alboreto's Ferrari F1-87 throws sparks after bottoming out on the asphalt at the 1987 Austrian Grand Prix in Zeltweg.

the next big step. In touch with Ferrari since his Formula 3 days, Alboreto joined the team in 1984, partnering with René Arnoux. The season started well enough with a win at the Belgian Grand Prix, but McLaren's Lauda and Prost quickly proved too dominant to beat. With a revamped technical team, Ferrari returned in 1985 with a much more competitive car. A thrilling battle between Prost and Alboreto captivated fans from the start of the season. Michele lost a near-certain win at Monaco due to a puncture but still dazzled with a remarkable second-place finish after a stunning comeback. He won in Montreal and Nürburgring, leading the championship heading into the final stretch. Unfortunately, Enzo Ferrari's decision to switch turbocharger suppliers led to a string of painful retirements, forcing Michele to concede the title. Despite everything he stayed loyal to Ferrari in 1986 but was given one of the worst cars in Maranello's history. In 1987, technical director John Barnard arrived from McLaren, but he never clicked with Alboreto, favoring Gerhard Berger instead. After two tough years, Michele's Ferrari chapter closed after six seasons. He was set to join Williams in 1989, but a last-minute deal fell through, and he returned to Tyrrell. Though resources were limited, the reunion revitalized both driver and team. Sixth in

Michele Alboreto with the Tyrrell-Cosworth 011, in which he won the second United States Grand Prix of 1983 on Detroit's downtown street circuit

Monaco and third in Mexico, Alboreto attracted a new sponsor he wasn't fond of, which ultimately ended the partnership. The rest of his Formula 1 career saw him racing for less competitive teams like Arrows and Footwork—essentially the same outfit—before ending with Minardi in 1994. He later tried his hand in Germany's DTM with Alfa Romeo and in America's CART series. Driving prototypes for Porsche under Jost, he scored a major career highlight by winning the 24 Hours of Le Mans with Tom Kristensen and Stefan Johansson—a victory that eased the bitterness of a difficult period. Afterward, Audi signed him for the World Endurance Championship. Now a mature man, Michele balanced racing with his passion for planes, Harley-Davidsons, and America. A father to Alice and Noemi, he dreamed of another Le Mans win. Confident in his abilities, he even invited old F1 colleagues to race alongside him. On Sunday, April 23, 2001, friends saw him for the last time at Monza, competing in a Lamborghini. Two days later, while testing a new Audi at the Lausitzring for the upcoming 24 Hours of Le Mans, a slow tire deflation at over 186 mph (300 km/h) caused the car to lift, flipping into a concrete wall. At forty-four, possibly nearing retirement with his final French 24 Hours just weeks away, Michele Alboreto lost his life.

ELIO DE ANGELIS

Elio de Angelis seemed to have it all. Born into a wealthy Roman family, he was the son of Giulio, a renowned offshore powerboat champion. Handsome, well mannered, and an accomplished pianist, thanks to his father Elio grew up with a passion for motorsports. He began karting as a teenager, showcasing his talent and earning numerous victories, including the European Karting Championship in 1976. That year, he also ventured into single-seaters, which paved the way for his entry into Formula 3 in 1977. Driving a Chevron, de Angelis clinched his first victory in only his third race in the category, and he went on to secure the Italian Championship by edging out Piercarlo Ghinzani in the final race. His European Formula 3 debut was equally promising, finishing seventh overall, an impressive result for a rookie. In 1978, at the Monaco Grand Prix for junior single-seaters, de Angelis showcased his grit. Chasing down French driver Patrick Gaillard in the final laps, he aggressively overtook at the Loews hairpin, causing Gaillard to spin. De Angelis claimed victory in the most prestigious Formula 3 race, capturing the attention of Formula 1 team managers. Ferrari took note, inviting him to test their 312 T3 driven by Carlos Reutemann and Gilles Villeneuve. However, the discussions didn't progress. De Angelis moved to Formula 2, achieving modest results. His Formula 1 debut came in 1979 with Shadow, the team run by the enigmatic Don Nichols, a former CIA agent in Asia.

Elio was not yet twenty-one when he competed in Argentina, finishing seventh and making an impression despite Shadow's waning competitiveness. His enthusiasm and determination made up for his lack of experience, and his performance at the rain-soaked United States Grand Prix at Watkins Glen—where he finished fourth—cemented his reputation and caught the attention of Colin Chapman. The Lotus boss signed him alongside Mario Andretti. De Angelis repaid Chapman's faith with a second-place finish at the Brazilian Grand Prix and consistent performances, including fourth-place finishes at Imola and Watkins Glen, keeping Lotus afloat during a challenging season.

By 1981, Nigel Mansell had joined the team, and de Angelis had matured into a composed driver, leaving his youthful recklessness behind. Despite Lotus's lack of competitiveness, he maximized every opportunity, earning valuable points like a seasoned professional. The tumultuous 1982 season, marked by the tragic losses of Villeneuve and Pironi, saw de Angelis achieve his first victory at the Austrian Grand Prix. In a nail-biting finish at Zeltweg, he edged out Keke Rosberg's Williams by just 0.05 seconds. However, the switch to Renault engines in 1983 com-

Elio de Angelis wasn't just a skilled driver; he was also an accomplished pianist.

ELIO DE ANGELIS — *ROME 03-26-1958* — *MARSEILLE 05-15-1986*

GP ENTERED	*108*
F1 WINS	*2*
POLE POSITIONS	*3*

Elio's Lotus debut at the 1980 Argentine Grand Prix ended with a suspension failure and early retirement.

promised reliability, though improvements in 1984 allowed him to finish third in the championship behind the dominant McLaren drivers Lauda and Prost. Often accompanied by his father, Giulio, and siblings Roberto, Andrea, and Fabiana, de Angelis became a respected figure in the Formula 1 paddock. Known for his politeness and poise, he was not afraid to stand his ground against critics, including Denis Jenkinson, the veteran British journalist famous for winning the 1955 Mille Miglia with Stirling Moss. His charm extended beyond the track, where his German model girlfriend, Ute Kittelberger, was a popular presence. De Angelis enjoyed life off the track as well, wowing German TV audiences with a piano performance at a Grand Prix event. A talented composer, he once stated that, if not a driver, he would have pursued a career in music.

However, the arrival of rising star Ayrton Senna at Lotus in 1985 disrupted the harmony. At the Brazilian Grand Prix, de Angelis secured pole position, his radiant smile reflecting his joy after qualifying. When asked about Senna, whom many had described as

One of Elio's final appearances in a Lotus at the 1985 European Grand Prix in Brands Hatch

a force of nature, Elio quipped that, after an unpleasant winter, the Brazilian seemed more like a fleeting phenomenon—at least for that day. He countered Senna's first win in Portugal with his own victory at Imola, although it came after Prost's disqualification. Despite leading the championship mid-season, de Angelis was overshadowed by Senna's growing dominance within the team, thanks to a victory in Belgium and better overall results. Feeling undervalued at Lotus, he joined Bernie Ecclestone's Brabham team for 1986.

Unfortunately, the move proved disastrous. The Brabham-BMW was slow and unreliable, leading to an eighth-place finish and three retirements in four races. On May 15, during testing at Le Castellet, de Angelis's car likely lost a piece of its rear wing at approximately 167 mph (270 km/h), flipping and hitting the guardrail upside down. Though he suffered head and spinal injuries, it was smoke inhalation from the resulting fire that claimed his life hours later.

NELSON PIQUET

Three Formula 1 World Championships weren't enough to convince everyone of Nelson Piquet's greatness. His father, Estácio Gonçalves Souto Maior, was a doctor, Brazil's Minister of Health, and an excellent tennis player. Nelson initially followed in his father's footsteps on the tennis court but eventually switched to kart racing. His family was against his racing dreams, so he used his mother's maiden name, Clotilde Piquet, slightly tweaking it to "Piket" for his early competitions. In 1976, he raced in a Formula Super Vee he had bought from the Fittipaldi brothers, becoming the national champion. The following year, on two-time World Champion Emerson Fittipaldi's advice, he moved to Europe to compete in Formula 3. He won two races in the European championship before focusing on the British scene. Driving a Ralt, Piquet secured thirteen wins in twenty-six races, claiming the BP Formula 3 Championship and finishing second in the Vandervell series.

Less than two years after arriving on the Old Continent, Nelson made his Formula 1 debut. Ensign offered him a seat at the German Grand Prix, but in Austria, the Netherlands, and Italy he raced in an older McLaren under BS Fabrications, a privateer team. Bernie Ecclestone noticed his talent and gave him a shot in a third Brabham-Alfa Romeo at the Canadian Grand Prix. His performance impressed, and Ecclestone signed him to partner Niki Lauda in 1979. Although plagued with retirements, Nelson managed a standout fourth-place finish at the Dutch Grand Prix. When Lauda abruptly retired at Montreal, Piquet suddenly found himself as Brabham's lead driver. From that moment, the team transitioned from Alfa Romeo engines to Cosworth ones.

Piquet built a close partnership with chassis designer Gordon Murray, quickly leveraging every advantage, even outshining Lauda, who was nearing the end of his career. Though not yet an experienced driver, he capitalized on Brabham's competitive car in 1980, winning his first Grand Prix at Long Beach, followed by victories at Zandvoort and Monza. In 1981, Murray and Brabham developed a ride-height adjuster to illegally lower the car, enhancing ground effect. Before rivals caught on, Piquet used it to win in Argentina and San Marino at Imola. A victory at Hockenheim kept him in the title hunt until the finale in Las Vegas. Although Carlos Reutemann (Williams) was the favorite, gearbox issues slowed the Argentine, and Piquet's fifth-place finish secured his first World Championship.

In 1982, Brabham switched to turbocharged BMW engines,

Three World Championships are the calling card of Nelson Piquet, a driver who made history under his mother's surname. His father, a doctor, was also Brazil's Minister of Health.

NELSON PIQUET — *RIO DE JANEIRO 08-17-1952*

GP ENTERED	*204*
F1 WINS	*23*
POLE POSITIONS	*24*
F1 WORLD CHAMPIONSHIPS	*1981, 1983, 1987*

The beautiful and nearly unbeatable Williams-Honda 1987 helped Piquet secure his third championship title, beating teammate Nigel Mansell.

making for a tough season filled with retirements. Nelson still claimed a victory at the Canadian Grand Prix, despite suffering burns to his feet from an oil leak. The following year, he battled Alain Prost and Renault for the title. Amid controversy over high-octane fuel, later deemed legal, the Brabham-BMW allowed Nelson to clinch his second championship at the South African Grand Prix at Kyalami, finishing third after Prost retired.

Off the track, Piquet embraced life to the fullest. He married in 1976 and became a father shortly after, but he divorced while his son Geraldo was still young. A renowned bon vivant and playboy, Nelson also admitted to being lazy. While with Brabham, he married Sylvia Tamsma and had three children, though a brief separation resulted in another child with Belgian model Katherine Valentin, a fixture at F1 events.

Brabham's switch to Pirelli tires in 1985 didn't suit Nelson, despite a win at the French Grand Prix. By the season's end, he accepted Williams-Honda's offer, leaving Bernie Ecclestone's team for a car with championship potential. At Williams, Piquet used his technical and political skills to unsettle Nigel Mansell, accusing the team of favoring the Brit and even taking personal jabs at Mansell, calling him rude and mocking his wife. Their rivalry allowed Alain Prost to win the title that year. In 1987, af-

Piquet's ties with Honda led him to Lotus in 1988 and 1989, taking over Senna's seat. Here, he's driving in wet conditions at the 1989 Canadian Grand Prix in Montreal.

ter a massive crash at Imola sidelined Piquet—his car slammed into the wall at the Tamburello corner after a wing failure—he fought hard for points throughout the season. Despite Mansell's six wins compared to his three, Nelson's consistency won him his third World Championship.

Back home, he faced increasing competition from Ayrton Senna, his fellow Brazilian driver. Nelson didn't shy away from mind games, even spreading rumors about Senna's personal life, going so far as to insinuate that he was gay. One of Piquet's proudest moments came in 1986, when he passed Senna on the outside at the Hungarian Grand Prix's first corner. However, as Senna's star rose, Piquet's career declined. He joined Lotus in 1988 and 1989, with little success, before moving to Benetton for his final F1 seasons. Nelson managed three wins with Benetton, including his last at the Canadian Grand Prix. After leaving F1 in 1991, he tried his hand at the IndyCar Series but suffered a devastating crash at Indianapolis in 1992, breaking his ankles and feet. Back in Brazil, Piquet found success in business, particularly in satellite-tracked transportation. His son Nelson Jr. followed in his footsteps, racing for Renault in Formula 1 in 2008 and 2009. Restless as ever, Nelson married for the third time and had two more sons.

NIGEL MANSELL

One of England's most popular F1 champions, Nigel Ernest James Mansell is a shining example of perseverance and determination. The son of an engineer, young Nigel idolized Jim Clark and decided to pursue a career as a driver. He began racing in karts before moving on to Formula Ford, where he became the British champion in 1977. Although he won most of the races he entered, his career was almost cut short by a severe crash during a practice session at Brands Hatch, which left him with a broken neck. Doctors advised him to rest for at least six months, but he fled the hospital, ignoring the risk of permanent paralysis if he were injured again. By then, Nigel had met and married Roseanne, his lifelong partner. Together, they sold some of their belongings to fund Mansell's 1977 Formula Ford 1600 season, which he won. Just three weeks before his crash, Mansell had quit his job as an aerospace technician. Roseanne had unwavering faith in her husband's talent and didn't hesitate to mortgage their home to cover the costs of his Formula 3 debut. Though the start of his racing career wasn't promising, Mansell eventually caught attention and joined Dave Price Racing in 1979. In his second year of Formula 3, Mansell suffered another significant crash after a collision with Andrea de Cesaris at Oulton Park in September, breaking three vertebrae. Despite his injuries, when Colin Chapman invited him to test a Lotus Formula 1 car at Le Castellet, Mansell loaded up on painkillers and hid his condition to seize the opportunity. The test went well, leading to Mansell's appointment as Lotus's third driver in 1980 alongside Mario Andretti and Elio de Angelis.

It was a turning point in his career, as Chapman began to recognize the English driver's testing skills. After an unsuccessful stint in Formula 3 at Monte Carlo with a March, Mansell was signed by Ralt in Formula 2 to test the Honda engine. However, the highlight of the year was his Formula 1 debut at the Austrian Grand Prix with Lotus. His first encounter with F1 was a painful one, as a fuel leak in the cockpit caused him second-degree burns. Chapman promoted him to a full-time seat in 1981. His rookie season saw its ups and downs but culminated in a third-place finish at the Belgian Grand Prix. The Lotus founder's sudden death in December 1982 hit Mansell hard, robbing him of his mentor. Over the next two years at Lotus, Mansell showed flashes of speed, displaying courage reminiscent of RAF pilots in WWII. However, he struggled to match the consistency of his teammate, Elio de Angelis. In 1984, Mansell gained attention with his daring drive at Monaco in wet conditions. He was leading comfortably but pushed too hard and hit the barriers. His tenacity was unmatched, epitomized by his effort at Dallas, where he physically

Mansell's iconic mustache was a signature look, but as a driver, he'll always be remembered for his determination and immense bravery.

NIGEL MANSELL — *UPTON-UPON-SEVERN 08-08-1953*

GP ENTERED	*187*
F1 WINS	*31*
POLE POSITIONS	*32*
F1 WORLD CHAMPIONSHIPS	*1992*

pushed his car across the finish line after running out of fuel under the sweltering sun. A move to Williams marked another pivotal moment in his career. Powered by Honda engines, the team's cars grew increasingly competitive, and at the European Grand Prix at Brands Hatch in early October, he finally earned his first (and well-deserved) Formula 1 victory. He repeated the feat at the next race and became a title contender for the 1986 season. The Williams cars were the ones to beat, but Mansell's relationship with new teammate Nelson Piquet was fraught with tension. In the season finale, Mansell lost the championship by a single point after a dramatic tire blowout on the longest straight of the Adelaide Circuit. In 1987, he dominated the season and outperformed his teammate, claiming six victories to Piquet's three. Yet, it was the Brazilian who ultimately took the World Championship title.

Among other setbacks, Nigel collided with Senna in Belgium, lost a wheel bolt while leading in Hungary, and went off-track during qualifying for the Japanese Grand Prix, injuring his back yet again. Fans adored Mansell's bravery and determination, but his frequent outbursts and complaints were less appreciated by the press and industry insiders, including his boss, Frank Williams. After losing the Honda engines, Mansell did his best to stay competitive in 1988 before being signed by the Maranello team.

Nigel joined Ferrari, racing alongside Berger in his first year and Prost in his second, achieving three victories. These included a surprise win on his debut in Brazil and another stunning performance in Hungary in 1989, where he overtook

Above: Mansell found success with Williams after debuting with Lotus, earning his first Grand Prix win at the 1985 European GP at Brands Hatch.

Colin Chapman gave Mansell his first break in F1. The Englishman is pictured driving a Lotus in 1981 at Zeltweg, where he debuted a year earlier.

One of Mansell's most cherished victories came at Silverstone in 1992, driving the iconic red No. 5. It was celebrated by euphoric fans.

Senna against the odds. Italian fans nicknamed him "Il Leone" (the lion) for his indomitable spirit. Mansell didn't seem particularly happy in 1990, partnered with Prost, going so far as to announce his retirement at Silverstone. However, the allure of a strong Williams-Renault brought him back. In 1991, he claimed five more Grand Prix victories but lost the title to Senna due to reliability issues in his car. His rivalry with the Brazilian was intense. Beyond his passion for golf, Mansell practiced martial arts, and at Spa in 1987, he famously "pinned" Senna against the wall by grabbing him by the collar of his racing suit. Their duels were unforgettable, often marked by incidents and collisions. Finally, in 1992, Mansell capitalized on the Williams car's active suspension system to dominate the season and secure his first World Championship. His triumph at Silverstone, celebrated with a lap of honor among ecstatic fans, became iconic. However, with Prost joining Williams for 1993, Mansell chose to leave Formula 1 rather than share a team with the sneaky Frenchman, who used political tactics off the track. He moved to the US and won the CART Championship, coming close to victory at Indianapolis.

After Senna's tragic accident in 1994, Williams called Mansell back for four races, and he returned to the top step of the podium at the season-ending Australian Grand Prix in Adelaide. To everyone's surprise, in 1995, he signed with Ron Dennis's McLaren, despite their notoriously strained relationship. However, at forty-one years old, Mansell retired for good after just two races. A father of three—Leo, Greg, and Chloe—Mansell owns the Woodbury Park golf course in Devon, having played golf at a near-professional level for much of his life. Once known for his signature mustache (which he has since shaved), he is now an avid cyclist and amateur magician. He even made a brief return to racing, participating in the 2010 24 Hours of Le Mans with Leo and Greg, though they retired after just five laps.

Above: The chaotic start of the 1989 French GP at Le Castellet, with Gugelmin's Leyton House flying over Mansell's Ferrari

ALAIN PROST

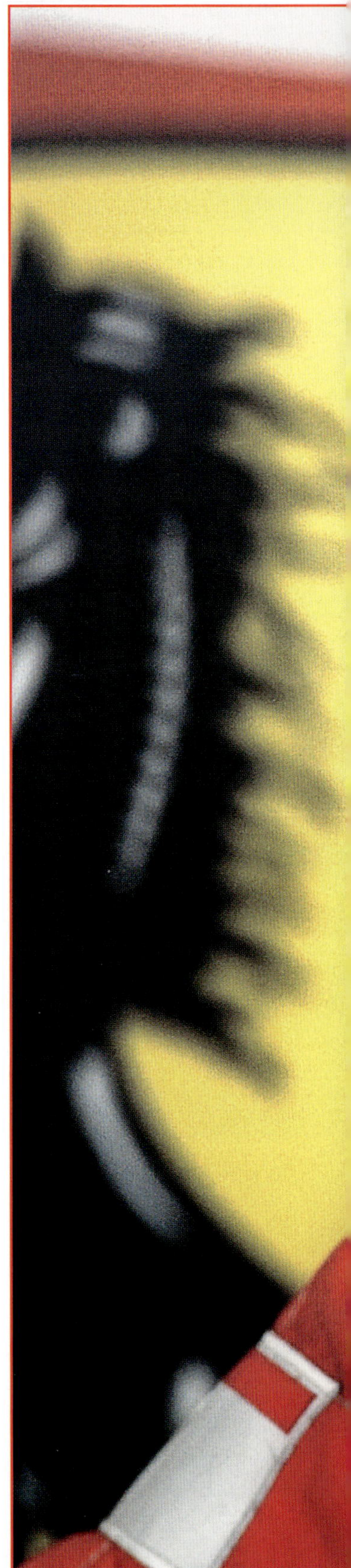

The most successful French racing driver of all time, Alain Prost, was born in the Loire region. As a youngster, he was a talented soccer player with the potential to compete at higher levels. At fourteen, during a vacation in southern France, Alain Marie Pascal Prost discovered karting, and by 1975, he became the French champion, funding his passion by selling karts and tuning engines. He continued climbing the ranks in Formula Renault, immediately dominating the French Championship in 1976 with twelve wins in thirteen races. In 1977, he won the more advanced Formula Super Renault category, paving the way for a move to Formula 3.

In 1979, Prost dominated both the national and European Formula 3 championships, driving a Martini-Renault and claiming victory at Monte Carlo. His transition to Formula 1 was inevitable, and it was McLaren that signed the small Frenchman with a sharp nose. Prost quickly gave seasoned teammate John Watson a run for his money, scoring his first F1 point with a sixth-place finish in Argentina, followed by fifth in Brazil. Alongside a couple of other point-scoring finishes, he also endured several crashes due to his car's fragility. He broke his wrist in Kyalami and injured himself again at Watkins Glen. Swearing never to race for McLaren again, he signed with Renault in 1981 to team up with René Arnoux. Prost secured his first Grand Prix victory at Dijon, France, adding wins in the Netherlands and Italy. In 1982, he started strong with two victories, but these were the only highlights in a season marred by disagreements with Arnoux, who left for Ferrari at the year's end.

Known for his speed, Prost also excelled off the track. A meticulous perfectionist with a passion for mechanics, he double-checked every detail of his car. At Renault, he began influencing team strategy, sometimes getting entangled in politics and conflicts with teammates. In 1983, Prost and Renault lost the championship in the final race after battling Nelson Piquet's Brabham-BMW all season. Alain won four races to Piquet's three but suffered an engine failure at Kyalami. He had made enemies within Renault and became the scapegoat for the defeat.

At the end of the season, Prost returned to McLaren, now under Ron Dennis's management, and moved to Switzerland with his wife, Anne-Marie—whom he had married in 1980—and their newborn son, Nicolas. At McLaren, Prost teamed up with Niki Lauda and began consistently outpacing him. However, controversy struck at the Monaco Grand Prix when race director Jacky Ickx prematurely ended the rain-soaked race just as a young Ayrton Senna was closing in on him. Prost won but received only 4.5 points instead of the usual 9 since the race had been cut short. The season unfolded with Niki focusing on race-day setups while Alain

The Ferrari could be a challenge for anyone. Even Alain Prost, despite five victories in 1990, ended his relationship with the Maranello team on a sour note.

FOSTERS
GOODYEAR
SEGA
RENAULT
CAMEL
elf
Labatt's
CHAMPION
KicKers

Left: Prost celebrates second place at the 1993 Australian Grand Prix podium, his final F1 race. He retired as the reigning World Champion.

Right: The Frenchman driving a Renault in 1981, the year he secured the first victories of a career that would ultimately see him achieve a total of fifty-one wins

dominated in qualifying, though his efforts sometimes ended in race retirements. At the decisive Grand Prix in Estoril, Lauda was crowned champion by just half a point, finishing second behind Prost. That razor-thin margin may have made Prost regret Monaco's early finish, where a second-place finish would have earned him six points.

The defeat made Prost mature, teaching him a valuable lesson. He became even more meticulous and analytical in tuning the car. Dubbed "the Professor" for his strategic acumen, Prost's hard work paid off in 1985 when he claimed his first world title. The following year, partnered with Keke Rosberg, Prost observed how the Finnish driver, while sometimes faster in qualifying, struggled to keep pace during the race.

With a series of timely podiums and victories, Alain surprisingly clinched the 1986 World Championship against the faster Williams cars. Prost worked seamlessly with his engineers, excelling at fine-tuning the car to suit his needs and optimize race strategy. Like Stewart, his philosophy was to win while driving as slowly as possible. Stefan Johansson, his teammate in 1987, was astonished by Prost's ability to provide detailed feedback and insights to the technical team.

In 1988, McLaren switched to Honda engines, and Senna joined the team. Ayrton was blisteringly fast, especially in qualifying, and Alain was smart enough to recognize it immediately. Instead of trying to outpace him in qualifying, Prost, much like Lauda had done four years earlier, focused on race-day setups. That year, Senna claimed the championship in a season where McLaren missed out on victory only at the Italian Grand Prix in Monza. The following year, their rivalry erupted, especially after Senna ignored a prearranged agreement at Imola by overtaking

ALAIN PROST	*LORETTE 02-24-1955*
GP ENTERED	*199*
F1 WINS	*51*
POLE POSITIONS	*33*
F1 WORLD CHAMPIONSHIPS	*1985, 1986, 1989, 1993*

Prost at the second corner. In the Japanese Grand Prix, the two collided, and Senna was disqualified, handing the title to Prost. Throughout the year, tensions ran high, with Prost accusing Honda of openly favoring the Brazilian. Alain had already announced his move to Ferrari, and in 1990, the two would face off as rivals. Back in Japan, Prost needed a win to keep his title hopes alive. Senna started on pole but from the unfavorable side of the track and got off to a poor start. Once behind Prost, he deliberately collided with him, securing his second championship. Prost's tenure at Ferrari didn't live up to expectations. In 1991, things went so poorly that the team fired him before the season ended. Taking a sabbatical in 1992, Prost returned with Williams in 1993, replacing Mansell and clinching his fourth World Championship ahead of his perennial rival, Senna. With the Brazilian set to join Williams the following year, Prost chose to retire, stepping away with fifty-one victories and four world titles, rather than face another season as his teammate.

In May 1990, Prost's second child, Sacha, was born, but he soon separated from his wife, Anne-Marie. His new partner, Bernadette—formerly married to fellow driver Jacques Laffite—gave birth to a daughter in 1996. A passionate cyclist, Alain also became a television commentator for French coverage of the Grand Prix before taking over the Ligier team in 1997. Renamed Prost Grand Prix, the venture struggled and eventually shut down in early 2002. Prost returned to racing on ice, winning the Trophée Andros multiple times between 2006 and 2012. Later, as a Renault ambassador, he began supporting his son, Nicolas, who competes in top-tier motorsport categories.

Above: The intense 1990 season saw Prost battle Senna for the championship. Their infamous collision at Suzuka sealed the title for Senna.

The tumultuous partnership between Prost and Senna at McLaren produced some of the most iconic moments in F1 history.

BOSS
MEN'S FASHION

AYRTON SENNA

Perhaps no other driver in history has been as consumed by the desire to be the best, the fastest, and the greatest at all costs. The career of Ayrton da Silva, who would later adopt his mother Neide's surname, Senna, began at the tender age of four, when his father, Milton, gave him his first kart, powered by a one-horsepower engine. He started racing karts seriously at thirteen, winning titles in Brazil and becoming runner-up in the World Championships in 1979 and 1980. Even then, he was a perfectionist, training until sunset and spending hours disassembling and cleaning his kart. In 1981, Van Diemen signed him to compete in Formula Ford 1600, and his debut in single-seaters was spectacular—he won twelve of nineteen races and claimed the championship. The following year, he competed in both the British and European Formula Ford 2000 series, quickly building a strong reputation. At Hockenheim, the entire Formula 2 paddock stopped to watch a supporting race featuring a new sensation named Ayrton Senna da Silva. Around this time, he began using his mother's surname, as he found his father's last name too common. Senna moved to England with his wife, Lilian, whom he had known since his youth, but their marriage didn't last long. She struggled with life in the UK, while Ayrton had only one true passion: racing and becoming the best. In 1983, he faced off against Martin Brundle in the British Formula 3 Championship, both driving similar Ralt cars. With twelve wins in twenty races, Senna was ultimately crowned champion.

The path to Formula 1 was now open. After testing for Williams and McLaren, he opted for Toleman in 1984. At his second Grand Prix in South Africa, he scored his first point, but it was at Monaco that he made a lasting impression. In pouring rain, Ayrton climbed from thirteenth on the grid to second in under twenty laps. He was catching leader Prost at four seconds per lap when the race was prematurely stopped, denying him what seemed like a certain victory. Along with his second place in Monaco, he added third-place finishes in Britain and Portugal. At the end of the year, realizing he couldn't win with Toleman, he bought out his contract and joined Lotus.

In the second race of the 1985 season, the Portuguese Grand Prix, Senna stood atop the podium after a rain-soaked victory. His speed in the wet was unparalleled, thanks to years of kart training in challenging conditions and his habit of walking the track to find the best lines. With Lotus, he won two races in 1985, two in 1986, and two more in 1987, when the team switched from Renault to Honda engines. Despite sixteen pole positions, his dream of becoming World Champion remained out of reach.

The opportunity came in 1988 with his move to McLaren-Honda, where he teamed up with Alain Prost. Senna wasn't just

Senna's desire to be the best drove him to constantly push his limits and strive for perfection.

AYRTON SENNA — *SÃO PAULO 03-21-1960* / *BOLOGNA 05-01-1994*

GP ENTERED	*161*
F1 WINS	*41*
POLE POSITIONS	*65*
F1 WORLD CHAMPIONSHIPS	*1988, 1990, 1991*

CHAMPION
John Player
John Player Special
DeLonghi
12
elf
GOODYEAR
Turbo RENAULT
MICROMAX
EAGLE

looking to beat Prost; he wanted revenge for the "theft" at Monte Carlo four years earlier. At the very same circuit, Senna secured pole position by an astounding 1.4 seconds over Prost. In the race, he built a lead of nearly a minute, but still pushing hard—perhaps trying to lap Prost—he crashed into the barriers exiting Portier. In a season completely dominated by McLaren, Senna prevailed with eight wins to Prost's seven, though the battle for the title was more decisive than the numbers suggested. Tensions between the two escalated in 1989. At Imola, driven by his unrelenting thirst for victory, Senna overtook Prost at the first corner, breaking a pre-race agreement. Prost was furious, and open war ensued. At the penultimate race in Japan, Prost was leading the championship, with Senna closing in. Senna attempted an almost impossible overtake—unless Prost allowed him to pass. Prost defended, and the two collided. Senna rejoined the track by cutting the chicane and went on to win, only to be disqualified. Prost was crowned World Champion. Enraged with the FIA and its French president, Balestre, Senna considered retiring but returned the following year, this time with Gerhard Berger as his teammate and Prost at Ferrari. A year later at Suzuka, Senna deliberately rammed Prost at the first corner, crushing his hopes of clinching the 1990 title with Ferrari.

Senna clinched his third World Championship in 1991 with McLaren-Honda, alongside teammate and loyal friend Gerhard Berger. By the time they reached Suzuka, Senna had already secured the title and decided to gift the victory to Berger, but instead of being discreet, he visibly slowed down before the finish line. Once again, Senna's need to assert his dominance had taken over. Ayrton struggled during the 1992 season, dominated by Mansell's stellar Williams-Renault. Holding Mansell off at Monaco brought him immense satisfaction, but being overtaken elsewhere visibly frustrated him, leading to some less-than-friendly remarks about the Brit. For Senna, being passed on track stung worse than a punch to the face. For journalists, though, he was a gold mine. Always outspoken, Senna was fluent in Portuguese, English, Italian, and French, and he had no shortage of opinions. Off the track, he could be a generous and compassionate individual, deeply moved by the struggles of the less fortunate—a reflection of his strong religious faith. Brazilians adored him, and he never failed to wave his country's flag after a victory.

With Lotus, Senna secured his first Grand Prix victories in 1985. Here he is pictured, the following year, at Imola in the Renault-powered 98T.

In 1993, McLaren had to settle for Ford engines, and Ayrton signed a race-by-race contract with Ron Dennis. Prost, now at Williams in place of Mansell, was once again his main rival. Despite his car's limitations, Senna managed to win five Grands Prix that year. At Donington—in the rain, of course—he delivered one of his most spectacular victories, overtaking four cars on the very first lap. While he benefited from traction control and a less powerful engine better suited to those conditions, Senna humiliated Prost and Damon Hill in an unforgettable race.

In 1994, he finally joined Williams, convinced he would reclaim the World Championship title. However, things didn't go as planned. Schumacher's unexpectedly competitive Benetton had already won the season's first two races as the team headed to Imola for the San Marino Grand Prix. Already marred by the death of Roland Ratzenberger during qualifying, the weekend took an even darker turn. During the race, while leading after the safety car period, Ayrton lost control of his car—likely due to a steering column failure—and crashed into the wall at Tamburello corner. Tragically, a suspension rod pierced his helmet near the eye, bringing an untimely end to the career and life of one of motorsport's greatest champions. It was a heartbreaking conclusion to a difficult time for Ayrton, who was facing immense pressure from Renault and disapproval from his family over his relationship with Adriane Galisteu. That evening, she waited in vain at the stunning villa Ayrton had recently purchased in Cascais, Portugal.

Above: Senna with Gerhard Berger, the only teammate who was also a friend. The two played outrageous pranks, including one where Ayrton's briefcase was thrown from a helicopter.

Right: In 1991, Senna won his third championship with McLaren. Here he is pictured at Phoenix during the season-opening United States Grand Prix.

Marlboro
COURTAULDS
Shell
COURTAULDS
Shell
Marlboro
HONDA
1
TAG HEUER
Shell
Shell

MIKA HÄKKINEN

Officially named Mika Pauli Häkkinen, complete with the umlaut on the "a," he became one of Michael Schumacher's fiercest rivals and a two-time World Champion. Häkkinen epitomized the classic Finnish demeanor, even in appearance. As a child, his father introduced him to karting, which led to an immediate crash. Determined to race again, young Mika relentlessly pestered his parents until they relented. At the age of seven, he clinched his first victory—a stepping stone in a long and successful career that eventually saw him crowned national and Nordic champion. His talent caught the attention of Keke Rosberg, the 1982 Formula 1 World Champion, who took Mika under his wing.

Racing in karts and mastering difficult grip conditions helped hone Häkkinen's skills, setting the stage for his motorsport career. In 1987, driving a Reynard in Formula Ford 1600, he claimed both the Nordic and Finnish championships. By 1989, he was crowned Formula Opel Lotus champion, and the following year, he won the British Formula 3 title in a Reynard. That same season, Häkkinen had his first memorable encounter with Michael Schumacher. Competing at the prestigious Macau Grand Prix, Mika secured pole position and won the first heat, but in the second, he collided with Schumacher, who went on to win while Mika retired.

Shadowed closely by Didier Coton, the manager assigned to him by Rosberg, Häkkinen made his Formula 1 debut in 1991, behind the wheel of a Lotus. Despite the car being far from performant, he miraculously secured fifth place at Imola in just his third race. Luckily for him, the English team developed a slightly more competitive car in 1992, thanks in part to switching from Judd to Ford engines. Mika regularly scored points, catching the attention of Ron Dennis. With Honda's departure, in 1993 McLaren had to resort to Ford engines, prompting Dennis to recruit Michael Andretti, Mario Andretti's son, due to his ties with the automaker and its motorsport division. Drawn, like many of his countrymen, to the allure of Scandinavian drivers, Dennis offered Häkkinen a role as a third driver. Though primarily focused on testing, Mika also competed in the Porsche Supercup at Monte Carlo. Driving a highly specialized car that demanded exceptional synergy for optimal performance, Häkkinen amazed everyone by defeating all the championship specialists, under the watchful eyes of F1 managers. Ron Dennis was thus eager to see him race in Formula 1. Michael Andretti, perhaps unfairly, wasn't in Dennis's good graces. After the Italian Grand Prix at Monza, and right after signing a contract with Peugeot, he was dropped to make room for Häkkinen. Mika immediately made an impression at Estoril, Portugal, outqualifying Ayrton Senna by a tenth of a second. Though he went off the track during the race, he rebounded in Japan with a third-place finish behind Senna, who claimed victory.

Mika Häkkinen was the second Finn, after Keke Rosberg, to win the World Championship, doing so with McLaren in 1998.

MIKA HÄKKINEN	*VANTAA 09-28-1968*
GP ENTERED	*161*
F1 WINS	*20*
POLE POSITIONS	*26*
F1 WORLD CHAMPIONSHIPS	*1998, 1999*

In 1994, when the Brazilian moved to Williams, Häkkinen became McLaren's lead driver. However, he was disappointed both by the car and the Peugeot engine's performance. At Hockenheim, he caused a crash at the start, which earned him a suspension for the next Grand Prix in Hungary. The season ended on a high note, with several podium finishes before McLaren switched to Mercedes engines in 1995.

Victory continued to elude him, but Häkkinen managed two second-place finishes at Monza and Suzuka amid several retirements. A dramatic turn of events came during the 1995 Australian Grand Prix in Adelaide, where a tire failure caused Häkkinen's car to crash violently into a concrete wall. While he was unconscious, his life was saved by an emergency tracheotomy performed trackside. Häkkinen was in a coma but gradually recovered, supported by his fiancée, Erja Honkanen, who was seven years his senior and guided him through rehabilitation. While he fully recovered, Häkkinen sustained partial hearing loss. Ron Dennis also provided unwavering support during this challenging period. By the start of 1996, Häkkinen was back to his usual pace. Despite a lackluster season, he secured his first Grand Prix victory at the European Grand Prix in Jerez in 1997, following the infamous collision between Schumacher and Jacques Villeneuve.

Known for his aggressive racing style, Häkkinen was shy and reserved off the track. He spoke sparingly and chose his words carefully. Always polite and composed, he rarely revealed his emotions. Since 1991, he had lived in Monte Carlo,

Häkkinen's McLaren-Mercedes surrounded by mechanics during the critical moments of a pit stop (tire changes and refueling) during a Grand Prix

Häkkinen exiting the pits during the 2000 Belgian Grand Prix, which he won after a stunning overtake on Schumacher

Left: Celebrating a win has its rituals, and in Budapest in 2000, Mika endured a champagne crossfire from Schumacher and Coulthard.

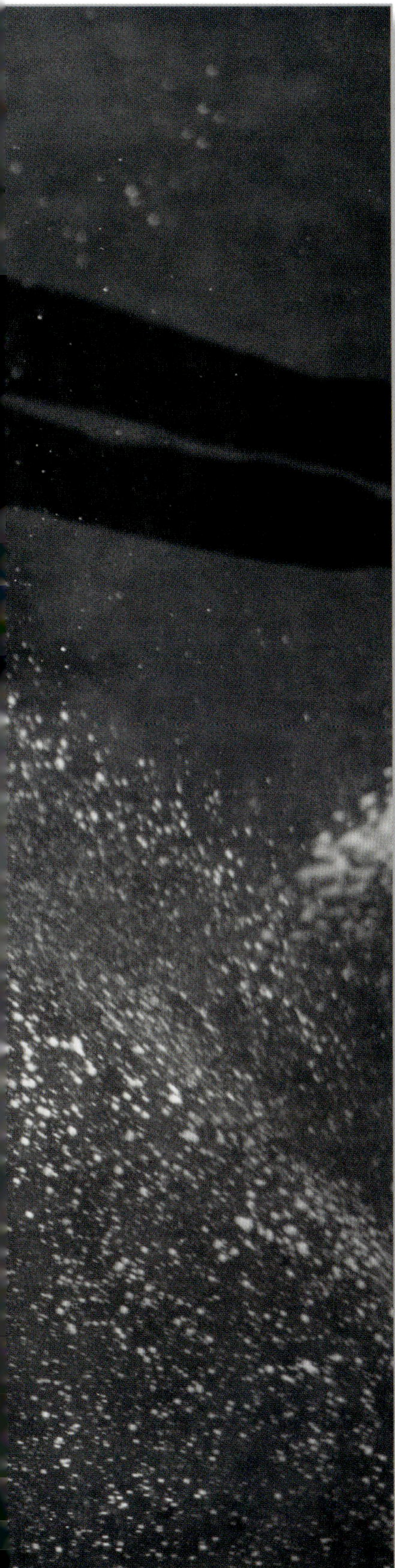

where he felt at home, with Erja and their pet tortoise. In 1998, McLaren-Mercedes finally gave Häkkinen a competitive car. He won eight races to Schumacher's six, securing his first World Championship. In 1999, after Schumacher's injury at Silverstone, Häkkinen had to fend off Ferrari's other driver, Eddie Irvine, to claim his second title. In 2000, Häkkinen lost the championship to Schumacher despite winning four Grands Prix, including an unforgettable victory at Spa, with a legendary overtake on his rival at the end of the circuit's longest straight. In 2001, a string of retirements quickly took him out of title contention. However, he still managed wins in the UK and the US, bringing his career tally to twenty F1 victories over five seasons with McLaren. Häkkinen married Erja in 1998, and the couple welcomed their son, Hugo, two years later. At the end of 2001, he announced he would take a year off from racing, but he never returned to Formula 1. In 2005, his daughter Aina Julia was born, and Häkkinen made a comeback in the DTM with Mercedes, where he competed until 2007, earning three victories. After retiring from racing for good, Häkkinen divorced Erja and began a relationship with Czech model Markéta Remešová, with whom he has had three more children, including twins.

Above: In 2000, in Spain, Häkkinen returns the favor, soaking Barrichello with champagne. That year, Häkkinen was Schumacher's toughest rival for the title.

1
TECHNOGYM
Mobil

MICHAEL SCHUMACHER

The career of the most successful driver in Formula 1 history started at a karting track run by his father in Kerpen, near Cologne. He began driving at the age of four and won his first karting championship at six. Despite the family's limited resources, Michael progressed thanks to a motorsport enthusiast, Jürgen Dilk, who supported him financially. He won races and championships in Germany before claiming the European titles in 1985 and 1987. In 1988, he made his mark in Formula Ford 1600 and Formula König, winning the German championship in the latter. Moving to Formula 3 demanded a bigger budget, but team manager Willi Weber gave him a seat. After a second-place finish in 1989, Michael won the national title the following year and capped the season with a victory at the prestigious Macau Grand Prix.

Schumacher's next step came with Mercedes, which established a junior team to compete in the World Sportscar Championship. Michael was chosen alongside Heinz-Harald Frentzen and Austrian Karl Wendlinger. At his debut in late 1990, he stood atop the podium alongside veteran Jochen Mass. His time with Sauber-Mercedes helped him mature as a driver, learning to manage powerful, heavy cars and their tires and brakes. He ended the season with a win in Japan, partnered with Wendlinger, but faced controversy at the Nürburgring when he intentionally collided with Derek Warwick's Jaguar. The British driver chased him into the paddock but refrained from hitting him after realizing Michael was as young as his own brother. By the time Schumacher won at Autopolis, he was already a rising star. His big break came when Bertrand Gachot was arrested in London, leaving his Jordan seat vacant for the 1991 Belgian Grand Prix. With Mercedes backing, Michael tested the car at Silverstone days before the race and immediately impressed with his speed. His manager, Willi Weber, falsely claimed Michael knew Spa-Francorchamps well, securing him one of the most memorable debuts in F1 history. Despite burning out the clutch at the start, he qualified sixth on a track he had only seen as a spectator. If not for his early retirement, Schumacher might have won his first Grand Prix—a feat only Giancarlo Baghetti had achieved. Ayrton Senna won that race, but Andrea de Cesaris, starting behind Schumacher in the other Jordan, closed in on him toward the end.

Eddie Jordan's mistake was failing to immediately sign Schumacher. Days later, Flavio Briatore stepped in, and from the 1991 Italian Grand Prix, Michael officially raced for Benetton. In his first full season, Schumacher displayed maturity with a string of consistent finishes, culminating in his first win at

With his arm stretched toward the sky and fist clenched, Michael Schumacher's signature celebration perfectly captured the spirit of the seven-time Formula 1 World Champion.

MICHAEL SCHUMACHER — *HÜRTH-HERMÜLHEIM 01-03-1969*

GP ENTERED	*306*
F1 WINS	*91*
POLE POSITIONS	*68*
F1 WORLD CHAMPIONSHIPS	*1994, 1995, 2000, 2001, 2002, 2003, 2004*

MILD SEVEN
MILD
VEN

Spa—on a rain-affected track. In the 1993 season, dominated by Prost's Williams, Michael achieved several second-place finishes and another victory in Portugal. At Benetton, Schumacher benefited from a close-knit technical team that included Rory Byrne, Ross Brawn, and Pat Symonds. Expectations were high in 1994, with Senna's Williams heavily favored. However, even before Ayrton's tragic accident at Imola, Schumacher had won the season's first two Grands Prix. His winning streak extended to six out of the first seven races, raising suspicions of traction control use. Schumacher was disqualified from two races for overtaking during the formation lap at the British Grand Prix and stripped of a win in Belgium for excessive wear on his car's wooden skid plate. Damon Hill closed the points gap, and the championship came down to the final Grand Prix in Adelaide. Leading the race, Schumacher hit a guardrail and rejoined the track, colliding with Hill's Williams and causing both to retire. Schumacher's first world title, the first for a German driver, remains controversial. Benetton switched to Renault engines in

Left: Michael driving the Benetton-Ford in 1994, the year he claimed his first title. Switching to Renault engines in 1995 made it easier to secure his second championship.

Above: In the pits at Interlagos, Brazil, Schumacher prepares for the tragic 1994 season, which he would go on to win.

In his early days with Benetton, Michael was more relaxed with the media and willing to pose, even for silly photos.

1995, making Schumacher's second title much easier. By then, Michael was living in Monaco and engaged to Corinna Betsch, formerly Heinz-Harald Frentzen's girlfriend. The two married in 1995. While adored by German fans, who nicknamed him "Schumi," Michael faced skepticism in the UK, where his reserved, sometimes aloof demeanor—a trait he attributed to his discomfort with public speaking—was harshly criticized.

In 1996, Schumacher moved to Ferrari, bringing Benetton's key technical staff with him. That year, he drove an ugly, heavy, and uncompetitive car but still pulled off the miraculous feat of winning three Grands Prix, including a masterful wet-weather victory in Barcelona.

The 1997 season ended in controversy as Schumacher, battling Jacques Villeneuve for the title at the European Grand Prix in Jerez, attempted to block Villeneuve's overtaking move, resulting in a collision. Villeneuve managed to finish fourth and secured the championship, while Schumacher was forced to retire and was disqualified from the standings.

Schumacher's quest for the title with Ferrari stretched on for several years. He finished second in 1998, but in 1999, he broke his leg in a high-speed crash at Stowe Corner during the British Grand Prix at Silverstone. However, after recovery, Schumacher and Ferrari became unstoppable, dominating from 2000 to 2004 with five consecutive championships, bringing

A young Schumacher in 1992 at Monte Carlo, discussing with Pat Symonds and Ross Brawn, the engineers who would join him at Ferrari a few years later.

his total to an unprecedented seven titles. In 2005 and 2006, his performance dipped, finishing third and second in the standings as Fernando Alonso claimed the crown. Protected by his team, Schumacher often appeared isolated and distant, an image further amplified by his intense ambition. Though reserved with the press—granting interviews and appearances sparingly—he was adored by his teammates and everyone he worked with. According to those close to him, his public persona was the opposite of his real character. One of his greatest strengths was his ability to analyze data and details during a race as if he weren't driving on the edge. Off the track, he worked harder than anyone to continually improve both the car and himself. Physical preparation was always one of his secret weapons, as he practiced various sports to maintain peak fitness. Perhaps not entirely convinced, Michael retired ahead of the 2007 season. By then, he was an incredibly wealthy man, a father of two—Gina Maria and Mick—living with his family in Switzerland on Lake Geneva, with homes in various parts of the world. He could do whatever he pleased, but it didn't take long for him to feel the void left by the thrill of competition.

He even tried his hand at Superbikes, risking serious injury in a nasty crash. For three years, he served as a consultant for Ferrari before receiving an offer from Mercedes, led by his old friend Ross Brawn. Rumor had it that he'd made some poor

SCHUMACHER
AMD
E

investments, which may have led to his falling out with longtime manager Willi Weber. While it's unlikely he needed the money, at forty-one, Michael returned to Formula 1. His prime as a driver was behind him, and the Mercedes car still needed significant development. Over three seasons, up to the end of 2012, the dream victory never came, though he held his own in direct competition with the young Nico Rosberg. Some argue that he could have avoided this comeback, but his only true blemish was an aggressive move against Barrichello at the 2012 Hungarian Grand Prix. The rest is more recent history, marked by a devastating skiing accident at the end of 2013 that left him paralyzed and requiring a long period of rehabilitation.

Left: As a tribute to Ferrari, Schumacher changed his helmet color to red. Here he is pictured in 2006, his final year with the Maranello team.

Above: Just a few drops of fuel leaking onto the exhaust during refueling was enough to ignite some flames—thankfully harmless—as seen here at the 2003 Austrian Grand Prix, which Schumacher won.

KIMI RÄIKKÖNEN

Only a driver with immense talent could make the improbable leap straight from Formula Renault to Formula 1. Born in Espoo, Finland, near the airport serving Helsinki, young Kimi Räikkönen was introduced to kart racing at the age of ten. Encouraged by his father, Matti, a road builder, he followed in the footsteps of his older brother Rami, who eventually reached Formula 3. With a Nordic Championship title and various karting successes, Kimi was quickly noticed by motorsport insiders, paving the way for his transition to single-seaters. In 1999, he debuted in the British Formula Renault Championship, immediately winning his first four races. The following year, he outdid himself, dominating the field with seven wins in ten races and clinching the championship title. His final tally was thirteen victories in twenty-three races—a record-setting performance in the category.

Kimi's exploits on British circuits caught the attention of David Robertson and his son Steve, who took the young Finnish talent under their wing. As skilled managers, they convinced Peter Sauber, head of the eponymous Formula 1 team, to give Räikkönen a test drive before the year ended. Despite having only twenty-three races in Formula Renault under his belt, Kimi tested a Sauber Formula 1 car at Mugello in September 2000, setting a time half a second faster than one of the team's regular drivers. Peter Sauber was immediately impressed.

Following additional winter tests, Kimi was signed by the Swiss team, though his lack of experience raised concerns. Sauber faced criticism from some FIA members, but they managed to secure a provisional super license for Kimi, which was contingent on his performance in the opening rounds of the season. Unfazed by the scrutiny and demonstrating the cool-headedness he would become famous for, Räikkönen scored points in his debut race with a sixth-place finish at the 2001 Australian Grand Prix.

From the start, Kimi displayed an almost detached attitude toward the Formula 1 paddock. For journalists, extracting more than a terse "yes" or "no" from him—even in response to detailed questions—was a challenge. His meteoric rise continued when he replaced Mika Häkkinen at McLaren in 2002. Likely to Ron Dennis's delight, Kimi's ice-cold demeanor earned him the nickname "Iceman," coined by the McLaren boss himself. His first victory, however, proved elusive during his initial season with the British team, as Ferrari and Michael Schumacher dominated the year. Finally, in 2003, Räikkönen secured his maiden win at the Malaysian Grand Prix. Consistent performances throughout the season saw him finish as runner-up in the championship, just two points behind Schumacher. Kimi's long stint with McLaren lasted until the end of 2006, yielding

Kimi Räikkönen in one of his final outings at Austin, during the 2023 NASCAR Championship

KIMI RÄIKKÖNEN	ESPOO 10-17-1979
GP ENTERED	349
F1 WINS	21
POLE POSITIONS	18
F1 WORLD CHAMPIONSHIPS	2007

Emirates
Henkel
SCHÜCO
JOHNNIE WALKER
Mercedes-Benz
JOHNNIE WALKER
SIEMENS

nine wins, including seven in the 2005 season, where he again finished second in the championship, this time behind Fernando Alonso. Married to the glamorous Jenni Dahlman—2001's Miss Scandinavia—Kimi began making headlines for occasional excesses. Reluctant to engage in public relations or interviews, he preferred to focus solely on racing. However, his undeniable speed earned him a call from Ferrari to replace Michael Schumacher in late 2006. Räikkönen's debut for the Maranello team was nothing short of spectacular. At the 2007 Australian Grand Prix, he secured pole position, the fastest lap, and the win—a stunning start to his Ferrari career. The season was marked by intense battles between Ferrari and McLaren, compounded by a scandal involving stolen technical data. Despite the odds and the arrival of Alonso, Kimi claimed five wins, including a pivotal victory at the penultimate race in China. Heading into the final round in Brazil, he trailed championship leader Lewis Hamilton, but a mechanical issue for the Briton opened the door. Kimi seized the opportunity, winning the race and clinching the World Championship title—the last for a Ferrari driver to date. The following two seasons brought limited success, with only three wins to his name, so Kimi left Ferrari and retired from Formula 1.

Unable to stay away from racing, he pursued a (distinctly Finnish) passion for rallying, competing in the 2010 and 2011 World Rally Championships with a factory Citroën. While he showed promise, the results were mixed—marked by solid results but also crashes—and the experience left him unsatisfied. He even dabbled in NASCAR in 2011. In 2012, Räikkönen made a surprise return to Formula 1 with Lotus, a team revitalized from the remnants of Renault. The Finn showed no signs of rust, finishing third in the championship and claiming a memorable victory at the Abu Dhabi Grand Prix.

The race became legendary for Kimi's radio response to his engineer, who was updating him on his lead over Alonso: "Leave me alone; I know what I'm doing." Always defiant of conventions, he underscored his rebellious streak by wearing a James Hunt-themed helmet at the 2012 Monaco Grand Prix. Räikkönen added another improbable victory at the 2013 Australian Grand Prix but ended his relationship with Lotus before the season's final two races, paving the way for his return to Ferrari. His second stint with the Scuderia

Discovered by Peter Sauber, who gave him his Formula 1 debut, Räikkönen joined McLaren after his first season with the Swiss team. Here he is in action at Imola in 2006, just weeks before announcing his move to Ferrari.

HUBLOT
HUBLOT
Santander

proved less fruitful, with only one victory at the 2018 United States Grand Prix and a third-place finish in the championship standings as his best result.

In 2019, Kimi moved to Sauber, rebranded as Alfa Romeo, where he spent three mid-field seasons before retiring from Formula 1 in 2021 after an impressive 349 Grand Prix entries. Meanwhile, after divorcing his first wife, Räikkönen remarried Minttu Virtanen, a Finnish former model, and they have three children. His eldest, Robin, has already started kart racing.

Left: Räikkönen driving the 2015 Ferrari during his second stint with the Maranello team. Despite numerous podiums, his only win in this period came at the 2018 US Grand Prix in Austin.

Above: The Finnish driver in the garage during practice for the 2017 Malaysian Grand Prix. That season, he teamed up with Sebastian Vettel, who secured five wins, while Räikkönen finished fourth overall with seven podiums.

STELVIO
CARRERA
Alfa Romeo
RICHARD MILLE

Left: Räikkönen's final Formula 1 season in 2021. He is pictured at the Emilia-Romagna Grand Prix in Imola, driving the Alfa Romeo Sauber. It was a farewell season with few highlights, yielding only four points finishes.

Above: A striking image of Räikkönen during the 2019 Monaco Grand Prix, driving the Sauber, which had been rebranded as Alfa Romeo that year. Strong results came early in the season, with eight points finishes in the first twelve Grands Prix.

Mobil 1
JOHNNIE WALKER
TAG HEUER
PIRELLI
SAP
Segafredo ZANETTI
14
JOHNNIE WALKER

FERNANDO ALONSO

José Luis Alonso, an explosives expert at a mine near Oviedo, always had a deep passion for racing and karting. It was thanks to him that Fernando Alonso, his son, got behind the wheel for the first time at just three years old. By seven, he was racing an actual kart. Always the youngest in his category, Fernando consistently outperformed older competitors, racking up wins with remarkable regularity. His rise was unstoppable, moving from national championships to claiming the world title in Gand in 1996.

Fernando caught the attention of Adrian Campos, a former driver who owned a Formula Nissan team. After testing him at the end of 1998, Campos debuted Alonso in the following season's championship. Fernando secured his first win in just his second race and ended the year atop the standings. In December 1999, Minardi put him in a Formula 1 car during a winter test session in Jerez. Alonso's performance was so fast it alarmed Cesare Fiorio, who called him back to the pits due to his blistering pace. By the day's end, Fernando was 1.5 seconds quicker than the other drivers who tested the car. In 2000, as the youngest participant in the Formula 3000 Championship, he finished fourth overall and won the final race at Spa.

In 2001, he made his Formula 1 debut with Minardi, a team not known for its competitiveness. Despite this, he outperformed his teammates and showcased a clean, highly efficient driving style. It wasn't long before Flavio Briatore and Renault signed him. In 2002, Alonso served as the third driver behind Trulli and Button. By 2003, he was part of the main team, exceeding expectations. At the Malaysian Grand Prix, only the second race of the season, he became the youngest driver in history to secure a pole position. Later that year, a month shy of his twenty-second birthday, he won the Hungarian Grand Prix in Budapest, again becoming the youngest race winner.

By then, Fernando had captured the world's attention. His boyish charm remained unchanged since his Minardi days. Living in Oxford to stay close to Renault's headquarters, he was perfectly positioned to capitalize on Michael Schumacher and Ferrari's declining competitiveness in 2005. With seven wins that year, Alonso beat Kimi Räikkönen and McLaren to become the youngest World Champion, breaking Emerson Fittipaldi's 1972 record. His evolution as a driver was evident, showcasing incredible race-reading skills, sharp tactics, and rapid adaptability. In 2006, Ferrari regained competitiveness, particularly toward the season's end, but Alonso still defended his title successfully, equaling Schumacher's seven Grand Prix wins.

Sporting a beard and a completely different look, Fernando Alonso returned to McLaren in 2015 after his previous stint with the Woking-based team alongside Hamilton in 2007.

FERNANDO ALONSO	*OVIEDO 07-29-1981*
F1 WORLD CHAMPIONSHIPS	*2005, 2006*

When he joined McLaren in 2007, his career seemed destined for more titles, but pairing him with rising star Lewis Hamilton proved problematic. The two clashed almost immediately during a season also marred by a spying scandal involving Ferrari and McLaren engineers. Both Alonso and Hamilton won four races that year, finishing tied with 109 points. However, Kimi Räikkönen's victory at the final race in Brazil edged him ahead with 110 points, crowning him champion. Alonso's relationship with McLaren soured, and he parted ways with the team at the end of 2007. He returned to Renault in 2008, securing victories in Singapore and Suzuka, although the first was tainted by teammate Piquet's deliberate crash, which brought out a timely safety car that benefited him.

Alonso finally joined Ferrari in 2010 after his staunchest critic, Jean Todt, left the team. This partnership, which seemed destined for success, saw Alonso narrowly miss the title at the final race in Abu Dhabi. In 2012, he had another chance, but Sebastian Vettel and Red Bull proved too strong. Alonso's tactical brilliance and consistent outperformance of teammates Felipe Massa and a returning Räikkönen were evident, but they weren't enough to clinch the championship. By the end of 2014, Alonso and Ferrari parted ways after years of highs

Above: The traditional team photo with all Renault staff and team principal Flavio Briatore after clinching Alonso's second world title at the 2006 Brazilian Grand Prix in Interlagos

Alonso driving the Renault R25, the car that secured his first World Championship in 2005, triumphing over Michael Schumacher's dominant Ferrari

and lows, often marred by the Spaniard's blunt and sometimes contentious demeanor.

Surprisingly, Alonso rejoined McLaren in 2015, burying the hatchet with Ron Dennis to spearhead Honda's Formula 1 return. However, an accident during winter testing forced him to miss the season opener, setting the tone for a disastrous year. His best result was a fifth-place finish in Hungary, and McLaren's lack of competitiveness limited him to mere points finishes in the following two seasons. In 2017, the team allowed Alonso to compete in the Indianapolis 500, where he was awarded Rookie of the Year before retiring due to engine failure.

After switching from Honda to Renault engines, McLaren's 2018 season remained disappointing. Meanwhile, Alonso pursued the World Endurance Championship driving Toyota prototypes starting that same year. A versatile

Above: Alonso behind the wheel of the McLaren-Mercedes MP4-22, in which he won four races during the 2007 F1 World Championship

Right: A stunning shot from Austin Tower shows Alonso during one of his final outings with Ferrari at the 2014 United States Grand Prix.

driver like few others, he managed to win the 24 Hours of Le Mans alongside Buemi and Nakajima. At the end of the year, Alonso retired from Formula 1 but continued racing with Toyota, winning Le Mans again in 2019 alongside the same teammates. He also attempted the Indianapolis 500, failing to qualify in 2019 and finishing far down the order in 2020. Never one to shy away from a challenge, he even competed in the Dakar Rally with Toyota.

In July 2020, Renault announced Alonso's return to Formula 1. Despite two years away from the Grand Prix circuits and driving an uncompetitive car, his comeback was promising. Numerous solid finishes, including a third-place podium in Qatar, highlighted the season. Renault fondly recalls his staunch defense against Hamilton in Hungary, which paved the way for teammate Ocon to secure victory. The following year brought more respectable finishes; however, tensions arose with Renault over the lack of a multi-year contract offer. Midway through the season, Aston Martin announced Alonso would join their ranks, yielding impressive results right from the start. His fourth-place finish in the championship, with eight podiums and two second-place finishes in Canada and Hungary in 2023, stands out as a crowning achievement in the latest chapter of Alonso's illustrious career.

Upon his return to Formula 1, Alonso joined Aston Martin after two years with Alpine. In 2023, he delivered an impressive streak of results, finishing second three times.

aramco
BOMBARDIER
ASTON MARTIN
JUNIPER
SentinelOne
Valvoline
BOSS
BOSS
BOSS
aramco
BANCO MASTER
14
NexGen
aramco

LEWIS HAMILTON

The first Black Formula 1 World Champion is the son of Anthony Hamilton, whose family immigrated to the United Kingdom from the island of Grenada in the 1950s. Anthony divorced Carmen, Lewis Carl Davidson's mother, when their future star driver was just two years old. At six, Lewis received his first kart for Christmas, on the condition that he behaved well at school. He debuted in karting at eight, immediately showcasing immense talent. By age ten, he claimed his first British karting championship, and at the year-end awards, he met Ron Dennis, head of McLaren. What happened next became legend: Lewis asked Dennis for an autograph and his phone number, introducing himself and confidently stating he would race for him one day. Amused, Dennis signed the autograph and added his number, telling Lewis to call in nine years.

The string of victories that followed, in every category Hamilton entered, ensured that it was Dennis who made the call, offering to sponsor Lewis's career and put him under contract. This happened in 1998, and the young talent's rise was almost unbelievable. By the end of 2000, he had become European karting champion and was named the best driver in the world—at just fifteen. At the close of 2001, he debuted in Formula Renault and became champion in his second full season, 2003, by a significant margin over his rivals.

His ascent to Formula 1 was marked by a Formula 3 Euro Series title and a win in the 2006 GP2 championship. At that point, Ron Dennis announced Lewis's entry into Formula 1 with McLaren, alongside Fernando Alonso.

Hamilton's debut was spectacular, finishing third behind Räikkönen and Alonso in Melbourne. The Spaniard won in Malaysia and Monaco, but Lewis responded with his first victory in Canada, which he followed up with another at Indianapolis just a week later. Alonso likely expected Hamilton, as a rookie, to support him, but things turned out differently. Their rivalry ignited, with Alonso accusing the team of favoring Hamilton. Both drivers ended the season with four wins, but Kimi Räikkönen claimed the championship in the final race by a single point over the McLaren duo. Displeased, Alonso negotiated his release from McLaren and returned to Renault.

In 2008, Hamilton thus became McLaren's lead driver. At twenty-three, he was more mature and aware of his talent. Some rivals claimed he was aggressive to the point of being unsportsmanlike, much like Senna had been years earlier. After all, Hamilton's yellow helmet was a tribute to the Brazilian legend.

Courage and determination were integral to Lewis's repertoire, earning admiration for his polite demeanor.

Meanwhile, his father had left his job to become his full-

A true karting prodigy, Hamilton won his first World Championship with McLaren-Mercedes in 2008.

LEWIS HAMILTON *STEVENAGE 01-07-1985*

F1 WORLD CHAMPIONSHIPS *2008, 2014, 2015, 2017, 2018, 2019, 2020*

Hamilton and teammate Nico Rosberg restored Mercedes to its 1950s glory, aided by the 2014 regulation changes.

time manager, a role some found overly intrusive. That season, Hamilton battled Ferrari's Felipe Massa for the championship, needing only a fifth-place finish in the final Brazilian Grand Prix to clinch the title. In a rain-soaked race, he only managed to recover fifth place in the final 300 meters, as Massa crossed the finish line victorious. At just shy of twenty-four years old, Hamilton became the youngest Formula 1 World Champion, breaking Alonso's record.

McLaren struggled in 2009 and 2010, yet Hamilton still shone with five wins over two seasons, including a stunning performance at Spa in 2010, dominating the track, opponents, and unpredictable weather. In 2011, for the first time, a teammate—Jenson Button—outperformed him in the championship standings, despite Hamilton's three wins to Button's two. He bounced back the following year, contending for the title until bad luck and crashes relegated him to fourth overall, though he still claimed four wins.

The partnership with McLaren seemed unbreakable, but too many seasons without a championship strained his relationship with Ron Dennis. Rumors circulated of heated arguments between the two. Ultimately, in late September 2012, Hamilton's move to Mercedes was confirmed, replacing Michael Schumacher and teaming up with Nico Rosberg. In his first year with Mercedes (2013), the car

Above: Hamilton's early days in Formula 1: The driver is celebrating his second-place finish at the 2007 Malaysian Grand Prix, just behind teammate Fernando Alonso.

Romain
RENAULT
EMAAR
burn
ZERO
PETRONAS
PETRONAS

was still no match for Red Bull or Ferrari; yet, Hamilton triumphed in Hungary and outscored Rosberg, who won at Monaco and Silverstone. Now resembling a rapper, complete with a pet bulldog, Hamilton indulged in his success, including purchasing a private jet for intercontinental travel.

With regulatory changes in 2014, Mercedes became the car to beat. The fierce competition between Hamilton and Rosberg leaned in Hamilton's favor due to his superior race pace. Hamilton's eleven wins to Rosberg's five secured his long-awaited second World Championship title. This was just the beginning of a dominant streak, with a third title following in 2015, again beating Rosberg. Their rivalry intensified in 2016, even leading to collisions, such as the infamous Spanish Grand Prix incident that eliminated them both. An unexpected engine failure at the Malaysian Grand Prix cost Hamilton crucial points, allowing Rosberg to win the championship.

However, that performance took such a toll on Rosberg that he retired at the end of the year without defending his title. Paired with Bottas, Hamilton capitalized on Mercedes's dominance, winning four consecutive championships (2017–2020), solidifying one of the most successful partnerships in racing history. In 2021, he faced a formidable rival in Max Verstappen, whose Red Bull team had made

Left: In his first year with Mercedes (2013), Lewis won only in Hungary. Pictured, Hamilton leading Grosjean's Lotus.

Above: Hamilton's and Alonso's McLaren-Mercedes cars line up for qualifying at the 2007 Malaysian Grand Prix in Sepang.

PETRONAS
Syntium
TeamViewer
IWC
AMG
SOLERA
Einhell
SAP
AKKODIS
PIRELLI
CROWDSTRIKE
INEOS

significant gains. Their battle lasted until the final race, controversially decided on the last lap when the safety car's premature withdrawal allowed Verstappen to overtake Hamilton, denying him an eighth title. Despite the uproar, Hamilton finished second in the standings. His previous victory in Saudi Arabia was his 103rd, a record that stood as Mercedes struggled in 2022 and 2023. However, Hamilton stunned the racing world by returning to the top step of the podium at Silverstone in 2024. He awaited a high-profile move to Ferrari at the start of 2025.

Left: Hamilton's Mercedes during practice at Monaco in 2024. That same season, two and a half years after his last win in Saudi Arabia, the British champion returned to the top step of the podium at his home Grand Prix at Silverstone.

Above: Hamilton holds the winner's trophy at the inaugural Saudi Arabian Grand Prix. It's 2021, his last victorious season with Mercedes before losing the championship in a controversial finale in Abu Dhabi.

SEBASTIAN VETTEL

Like many drivers of the newer generations, Sebastian Vettel started his career in karting—first in the backyard of his house in Heppenheim, and later competing in races at the age of seven. As a child, Sebastian was a huge fan of Michael Schumacher, whom he had the chance to meet during the awards ceremony of one of his early victories. His talent caught Red Bull's attention at just eleven years old, which helped him overcome the financial challenges that might have otherwise hampered his career. He secured major victories, including wins in Monte Carlo and Paris. Even before debuting in single-seaters, Sebastian showed remarkable intelligence in understanding the mechanics, fine-tuning the car, and developing race strategies. In 2004, at just seventeen, he dominated the German Formula BMW Championship, winning eighteen of twenty races. The following year, he competed in the European Formula 3 Championship, finishing fifth. That September, he had his first experience in a Formula 1 car, testing a Williams-BMW at Jerez. The year 2006 was pivotal in his career. Alongside competing in the continental Formula 3 series, Vettel became the third driver for BMW Sauber, then owned by the Munich-based brand. The team's support allowed him to relocate to Switzerland. At the end of that season, he finished as runner-up to teammate Paul di Resta in the European Formula 3 series.

The following year, his racing schedule revolved around competing in the World Series Renault, while continuing as BMW Sauber's third driver. When Robert Kubica was injured in a massive crash at Montreal during the Canadian Grand Prix, Vettel made his Formula 1 debut at the 2007 United States Grand Prix, qualifying seventh and finishing eighth. According to some within BMW Sauber at the time, Sebastian wasn't yet as fast as Heidfeld and Kubica, so when Toro Rosso approached him to replace American Scott Speed, the Heppenheim-born boy was released. Starting from the Hungarian Grand Prix, Vettel became a full-time Formula 1 driver, leaving the World Series midway through the season. Getting to grips with Toro Rosso, he impressed in a rain-soaked race at Suzuka. In that Japanese Grand Prix, he was running third behind Webber's Red Bull under a safety car. Unfortunately, an unexpected move by Hamilton caught Sebastian off guard, leading to a collision with Webber. Thankfully, just fifteen days later, he bounced back with a brilliant fourth-place finish in China.

Vettel felt at home with Toro Rosso. After a shaky start to the season with retirements and crashes, he overshadowed Sébastien Bourdais, who had come to F1 with a string of wins in the American Champ Car series. Finishing fifth at Monte Carlo, Vettel made significant progress in both car management and race strategy.

After winning four titles with Red Bull, Sebastian Vettel raced with Ferrari from 2015 to 2020.

SEBASTIAN VETTEL	*HEPPENHEIM 07-03-1987*
GP ENTERED	*299*
F1 WINS	*53*
POLE POSITIONS	*57*
F1 WORLD CHAMPIONSHIPS	*2010, 2011, 2012, 2013*

SCUDERIA
FERRARI
OAKLEY

bmw-sauber-f1.com
Pull
PETRONAS
DELL
Pull

The Italian Grand Prix at Monza was held in the rain, and to everyone's surprise, Vettel secured pole position in his Toro Rosso. In the challenging race conditions, he drove impeccably, claiming a stunning and well-deserved victory in the wet. That weekend, at just twenty-one years old, he became the youngest driver ever to achieve pole position and win a Grand Prix.

The transition from Toro Rosso to Red Bull was almost automatic in 2009, as he was chosen to replace David Coulthard. That year, the Brawn GP cars dominated thanks to a better understanding of the regulations, with Button clinching the championship. Still, Sebastian took four wins—in China, Japan, Great Britain, and Abu Dhabi—finishing runner-up. In 2010, the rivalry with teammate Webber flared up.

The Red Bull was the car to beat, but frequent mistakes and Alonso's consistency made the Ferrari driver a serious contender. In Turkey, Vettel collided with Webber while trying to take the lead, ending his race prematurely. Heading into the season finale in Abu Dhabi, Vettel's chances of winning the championship seemed slim. However, Webber—initially the favorite—pitted too early and got stuck in traffic, as did Alonso. With an undeniable victory, Sebastian became the youngest World Champion in history at 23 years and 133 days. Winning his second title in 2011 was almost a formality, but the following year was more challenging. He claimed his third title only at the season's final race in Brazil.

After being hit by Bruno Senna and sustaining significant car

Left: A beautiful overhead shot of the German champion in the cockpit of the BMW Sauber at Indianapolis in 2007. By the Hungarian Grand Prix, he had already moved to Toro Rosso.

Above: One of the iconic photos from Vettel's Formula 1 debut at Indianapolis in 2007. Called up as BMW Sauber's third driver, he replaced Robert Kubica.

On his way to his third World Championship, Sebastian takes on the undulations of the Austin Circuit during the 2012 US Grand Prix.

damage, Vettel recovered to finish sixth, securing the championship once again. In 2013, his fourth title capped another dominant year. But in 2014, regulation changes caused Vettel to struggle for the first time, and he was outperformed by his new teammate. Ricciardo's three wins may have influenced Vettel's decision to join Ferrari in 2015, aiming to emulate his idol, Michael Schumacher. Unfortunately for Vettel, Mercedes continued to dominate Formula 1. Still, in his first year with Ferrari, Vettel won three Grands Prix and finished third in the championship behind Hamilton and Rosberg. The following season was tougher, with 2016 seeing Vettel settle for seven podium finishes while defending against Mercedes's dominance. Ferrari was far more competitive in 2017, and Vettel won five races, finishing second in the championship. The same pattern repeated in 2018, with Hamilton as World Champion and Vettel again finishing as runner-up with five wins. The arrival of Charles Leclerc at Ferrari made life harder for Vettel within a team where driver pressure is exceptionally high.

The new Ferrari duo finished fourth and fifth in the standings, with Leclerc ahead thanks to two wins compared to Vettel's one. Sebastian's Ferrari chapter

Above: Vettel gives a unique thanks to Red Bull in 2013 after securing his fourth title on the finishing straight at the Noida Circuit in India.

cognizant ASTON MARTI
workday
aramco
crypto.com
cognizant
JCB
BOMBARDIER
PERONI
P ZERO
PIRELLI

ended after 2020, a year where Maranello's cars were astonishingly uncompetitive. Leclerc finished eighth in the championship, while Vettel dropped to thirteenth. Moving to Aston Martin alongside Lance Stroll didn't add much to Vettel's record, aside from a second-place finish at Baku in 2021. By the end of that year, the four-time World Champion—now a father of three with longtime partner Hanna, whom he's known since childhood—announced his retirement. A fan of the Beatles, Vettel also enjoys some British TV series. As a racing enthusiast, he treated himself to Mansell's 1992 Williams and Senna's 1993 McLaren, which he has driven at events in Silverstone and Imola.

Left: The German champion prepares for a pit stop during the Emilia Romagna Grand Prix in 2022. Even before the season ended, he announced his retirement with four World Championships under his belt.

Above: Vettel driving the Aston Martin in 2021, when he claimed second place in the Azerbaijan Grand Prix, his best result in two seasons with the British team

CHARLES LECLERC

With his clean-cut face and boy-next-door appearance, Charles Leclerc might once have been described as the son every mother dreamed of having, and Mrs. Pascale must surely be proud. Of her three sons, two—Charles and the youngest, Arthur—followed in the footsteps of their Monegasque father, Hervé, a solid Formula 3 driver during the 1980s.

Thanks to the family business founded by Charles's grandfather in the automotive parts sector, the young Leclerc was able to start karting at just seven years old. He wasted no time in making waves, becoming a regional champion three out of four years between 2005 and 2008. By 2009, Charles was already the French Cadet Karting Champion, the youngest to ever clinch the title. As he transitioned to more advanced karting categories, Leclerc's rise was unstoppable. He won the Junior KF3 class in Monaco and finished runner-up in the French series by the end of 2010. The following year, he captured the KF3 World Championship title. The trophy case kept growing: In 2012, he became the youngest European Champion in the under-18 KF2 class, and in 2013, he was second in the KF1 World Cup behind none other than Max Verstappen.

A move to single-seaters was the next logical step in his meteoric rise. In 2014, young Charles debuted in Formula Renault, earning two wins and nine podiums in the French-Italian championship. After finishing fourth in the European Formula 3 Championship, Charles turned heads by dominating in two of the most crucial stepping-stone series for aspiring Formula 1 drivers. As a Ferrari Driver Academy recruit, he clinched the GP3 championship in 2016 and followed it up with the Formula 2 title in 2017.

However, his journey wasn't without heartbreak. The first blow came with the passing of Jules Bianchi, who died after nine months in a coma following a tragic accident in his Marussia during the 2014 Japanese Grand Prix. Bianchi was a close family friend of the Leclercs, especially of Lorenzo, Charles's older brother. Many photos show the French driver with Charles, his godson, at various racetracks. Worse still, in 2017, just days before a Formula 2 race in Azerbaijan, Charles lost his father, Hervé, to a long illness. He passed away at just fifty-four, with the cold comfort of knowing his son was destined for Formula 1, although the Sauber contract wasn't signed until a month later.

A stellar karting and junior formula career propelled young Charles Leclerc to Ferrari in 2019.

CHARLES LECLERC *MONTE CARLO 10-16-1997*

Everyone who knows Charles well describes him as kind, polite, and empathetic. He quickly endeared himself to the Swiss F1 team, then led by Frédéric Vasseur, who had previously overseen Leclerc's GP3 triumph with ART. In his rookie F1 season with Sauber, Leclerc rapidly adapted to the big leagues, scoring points by the fourth race at Baku, Azerbaijan. Often claiming the top five qualifying positions, Charles earned points in ten races. This string of results and his composure behind the wheel earned him the title of Rookie of the Year and, more significantly, a contract with Ferrari alongside Sebastian Vettel. Driving for Ferrari was a massive challenge, especially alongside a teammate like Vettel, a seasoned champion with five race wins the previous year.

Left: A striking overhead view of Leclerc's Ferrari in the Spa-Francorchamps pits during the 2023 season, his fifth with the Maranello team

Above: An intense moment between Charles Leclerc and Lewis Hamilton during the 2023 Austrian Grand Prix. The Monegasque driver ultimately secured his best finish of the season with second place.

However, Ferrari's competitive cars allowed Leclerc to shine, even in a season largely dominated by Mercedes. By his second race in Bahrain, he grabbed his first pole position and finished third after leading much of the race. In Austria, he claimed second place after a heated battle with Verstappen, which included a controversial contact.

The speed of that year's Ferrari SF90 enabled Leclerc to secure pole position at Spa-Francorchamps on the eve of the Belgian Grand Prix. Masterfully converting his pole into a win, Leclerc earned his first career victory at Spa the following day. He followed it up with a win at Monza, becoming an instant hero on Ferrari's historic home turf. Further pole positions came in Singapore and Sochi, Russia, though he finished second and third, respectively. Leclerc ended the season fourth in the standings.

Above: Leclerc's signature red-and-white helmet is barely visible amid the cockpit protection of his Ferrari.

In 2023, Formula 1 raced through the streets of Las Vegas under dazzling lights. Here, Leclerc navigates his Ferrari through one of the circuit's tight corners.

Perhaps Leclerc's most meaningful victory came at his home Grand Prix at Monte Carlo in 2024, a tribute to his late father, Hervé.

In modern Formula 1, a driver's success is closely tied to the team's performance. Unfortunately for both Ferrari and Leclerc—as well as Vettel—2020 was an incredibly challenging year, with limitations on their engine due to alleged rule breaches in 2019.

Amid a COVID-affected calendar, Leclerc's best result was a second-place finish, and he ended the season eighth in the standings. The struggles persisted into 2021, though Charles, teamed up with newcomer Carlos Sainz, took pole at his home race in Monte Carlo and again in Baku. However, a second-place finish at Silverstone was his only podium of the season.

Ferrari's fortunes improved in 2022 with new regulations. Armed with a competitive car, Leclerc took eight pole positions

On the podium at Imola in 2024, Leclerc celebrates his third-place finish. Starting in 2025, he'll team up with Lewis Hamilton.

in twenty-two races and won in Bahrain, Australia, and Austria. He finished the year as runner-up to Verstappen in the championship standings.

However, 2023 was all about Red Bull dominance, leaving only one win for the competition—Sainz's victory for Ferrari—out of twenty-three Grands Prix. Leclerc endured a challenging year, though he managed five pole positions and three second-place finishes. In 2024, Ferrari's struggles persisted, but Leclerc delivered a stunning victory at the Monaco Grand Prix, his home race, after starting from pole. The win was deeply emotional for Charles, his mind flooded with memories of his father, Hervé, during the final laps of a triumphant drive. With his smooth and precise driving style, Leclerc continues to draw comparisons to Alain Prost.

MAX VERSTAPPEN

In the history of racing, the sons of legendary drivers have rarely lived up to their parents. Notable exceptions include Alberto Ascari and Hans-Joachim Stuck, though the latter achieved his greatest victories in prototypes rather than Formula 1 cars. Max Emilian Verstappen, however, is a double legacy, born to Jos Verstappen and Sophie Kumpen, a karting star with international recognition. Back in the late 1980s, Sophie raced alongside future champions like Jenson Button and regularly outpaced Christian Horner, who would later become Red Bull's F1 team boss.

Jos Verstappen could be described as a solid professional behind the wheel, best remembered as Michael Schumacher's teammate at Benetton in 1994, a year when he claimed two podium finishes with third places in Hungary and Belgium. Perhaps more famously (or infamously), Jos was caught in a fiery pit stop during the German Grand Prix at Hockenheim—a moment that fortunately caused more panic than harm. Without a doubt, Jos's true masterpiece is his son Max, whom he raised with almost military discipline. Little Max began karting at age four, spending time not only on the track but also with his father's illustrious friends, including none other than Michael Schumacher. Results came quickly: In 2005, Max clinched the Belgian Mini Junior Championship, winning all twenty-one races. This marked the beginning of a meteoric rise, scoring victory after victory, that culminated in a World Championship title in the KF1 category, where he beat Charles Leclerc.

His transition to car racing was equally impressive. At just sixteen, Max won two races in the 2014 Florida Winter Series, but that was only the beginning: He moved to Formula 3, competing in the European Championship the same year. As always, Max was blisteringly fast and determined. After five rounds, he stood on the top step of the podium and began a streak of six consecutive victories. By the end of the season, he had ten wins and finished third in the championship, also triumphing at the Formula 3 Masters at Zandvoort, a one-off event akin to a World Championship.

As his career skyrocketed, Max caught the attention of Toto Wolff and Mercedes, but in August 2014, he chose to join the Red Bull Junior Team.

Easy said, easy done. By 2015, he was racing for Toro Rosso, making him the youngest-ever Formula 1 driver. At 17 years and 166 days, Max debuted in Melbourne. Partnered with Carlos Sainz, he didn't disappoint, even in the high-pressure environment of F1. In only his second race, the Malaysian Grand

En route to his second World Championship, Verstappen hoists the winner's trophy at the 2022 Belgian Grand Prix.

MAX VERSTAPPEN	*HASSELT 09-30-1997*
F1 WORLD CHAMPIONSHIPS	*2021, 2022, 2023*

150 YEARS
Infinitum
citrix
RAUCH
inter.mx

ERSTAPPEN
Red Bull
WATER

Prix, Max finished an impressive seventh, becoming the youngest driver to score points in a Grand Prix. His fourth-place finish in Hungary capped a series of standout performances, earning him forty-nine points and an eleventh-place finish in the championship alongside a reputation as a once-in-a-generation talent.

However, Verstappen's rise didn't stop with the Toro Rosso team. When Daniil Kvyat was demoted from Red Bull to Toro Rosso after just four races in 2016, the main team welcomed the young Dutch champion with open arms. The results came instantly.

In his Red Bull debut at the Spanish Grand Prix, he took a stunning victory, becoming the youngest Grand Prix winner at just eighteen years and seven months. Driving a competitive car, Max became a fearless and relentless racer, drawing comparisons to Ayrton Senna, particularly for his exceptional car control—best exemplified in a wet race at Interlagos. Starting sixteenth, he climbed to third in the final fifteen laps, set the fastest lap, and earned admiration even from Mercedes's Toto Wolff.

Left: The Dutch driver's Red Bull during a pit stop at the 2017 Malaysian Grand Prix

Above: Max Verstappen debuted in Formula 1 as a minor, driving for Toro Rosso in 2015. By his fifth race the following year, he had been promoted to Red Bull, winning in Spain in his debut with the British team.

Championship at Suzuka in 2022

His second year at Red Bull, in 2017, began with challenges, including a string of retirements. Teammate Daniel Ricciardo won in Baku, but Max had the last laugh later that season with victories in Malaysia and Mexico. In 2018, amid continued established himself as "the best of the rest," winning three Grands Prix each season.

In 2021, with a renewed contract and a more competitive car, Verstappen's Red Bull finally challenged Mercedes head-on. It

In a 2023 season packed with victories—19 out of 22 Grands Prix—Verstappen celebrates his win in Japan.

by race director Michael Masi to only allow certain lapped cars to unlap themselves set up a one-lap shootout. With his fresher tires, Verstappen overtook Hamilton's Mercedes in the final lap, clinching his first World Championship amid widespread debate. The regulatory changes introduced in Formula 1 for 2022 gave Red Bull a significant technical advantage, solidifying their dominance.

Verstappen couldn't have asked for more, combining his undeniable championship-caliber talent with an almost unbeatable car in his hands. The results speak for themselves: two additional World Championships were secured after winning fifteen out of twenty-two races in 2022 and a record-breaking nineteen in 2023. The fourth title in 2024 proved more challenging. A shaky Red Bull struggled mid-season after a dominant start. However, a sensational win in wet conditions in Brazil, starting seventeenth, allowed Max to seal the championship with a solid finish in Las Vegas, outpacing rival Lando Norris during the third-to-last race of the season.

Above: The unmistakable hairpin at Monaco's Lower Mirabeau and Portier corners, navigated by Verstappen during the 2023 Grand Prix

Right: At the critical start of a Grand Prix, Verstappen battles Sainz's Ferrari. Driving the 2023 RB19, Max dominated the season and clinched his third World Championship.

Following pages: A close-up of the three-time World Champion during practice in Sakhir, Bahrain, just before the 2024 season began. The Verstappen-Red Bull partnership will go down as one of the most successful in Formula 1 history.

Mobil
BYBIT
RAUCH

ROKT
ORACLE
Mobil 1

About the Author

ROBERTO GURIAN, a professional journalist since the 1980s, began his career writing for automotive magazines before transitioning to freelancing. He currently collaborates with *la Repubblica*, *Auto*, and *AM*, with a focus on car reviews. For years, he has been a commentator for RSI, the Italian-language Swiss TV channel, covering Formula 1 Grand Prix. An amateur cyclist, he manages to ride nearly 5,600 miles (9,000 km) annually, keeping alive his lifelong passion for bicycles. A dedicated sports enthusiast, he follows disciplines ranging from ice hockey to skiing. In 2015, he published *Bicycles: Past, Present, and Future* with Edizioni White Star.

Photo Credits

Allsport UK/Allsport/Getty Images: 120–121
Samuel Aranda/Getty Images: 161
Cristiano Barni/Shutterstock: 176–177, 180–181, 181, 197, 205, 206, 208–209, 209, 210–211, 215, 217
Lars Baron/Bongarts/Getty Images: 193, 201
Barratts/S&G and Barratts/EMPICS Sport/Press Association/IPA: 74
Simon Bruty/Allsport/Getty Images: 138
Giuseppe Capace/AFP/Getty Images: 194
Robert Cianflone/Getty Images: 190
Colorsport/Colorsport/Corbis: 86
AlessioDeMarco/Shutterstock: 204–205, 220
Bob D'Olivo/The Enthusiast Network/Getty Images: 51
Terry Disney/Central Press/Getty Images: 26
Tony Duffy/Getty Images: 97
Silvio Durante/LaPresse Archivio Storico/LaPresse: 28, 37, 43
Fox Photos/Getty Images: 38
Getty Images: 203
Grand Prix Photo/Getty Images: 47
Bertrand Guay/AFP/Getty Images: 186
Handout/Getty Images: 182
Jay Hirano Photography/Shutterstock: 188–189, 196–197, 212, 218, 219, 220–221, 222–223
Bob Harmeyer/Archive Photos/Getty Images: 109, 126
Heritage Images/Getty Images: 18–19
Hulton Archive/Getty Images: 30–31
Jasper Juinen/Getty Images: 172–173
Keystone Features/Getty Images: 52
FiledIMAGE/Shutterstock: 210
Keystone-France/Gamma-Keystone/Getty Images: 14–15, 88
Klemantaski Collection/Getty Images: 2–3, 14, 31, 44
Michael King/Getty Images: 137
INP/Picture Alliance/IPA: 20
Imagno/Getty Images: 10–11, 16, 23
Hafiz Johari/Shutterstock: 216–217
LaPresse Archivio Storico/LaPresse: 41
Mauricio Lima/AFP/Getty Images: 184
Boris Lipnitzki/Roger-Viollet/Alinari: 12
David Lees/Picture Post/Hulton Archive/Getty Images: 34–35
Jean-Marc Loubat/Gamma-Rapho/Getty Images: 150
Clive Mason/Getty Images: 199
National Motor Museum/Heritage Images/Getty Images: 13, 41
Alexander Nemenov/AFP/Getty Images: 192–193
PA Archive/Press Association Images/IPA: 32
Popperfoto/Getty Images: 77
Michael Potts F1/Shutterstock: 213
RacingOne/Getty Images: 24
Abdul Razak Latif/Shutterstock: 179
Reporters Associes/Gamma-Rapho/Getty Images: 87
Rolls Press/Popperfoto/Getty Images: 71
Pascal Pavani/AFP/Getty Images: 166
Mike Powell/Getty Images: 142
Logan Riely/Getty Images: 174
Pascal Rondeau/Getty Images: 141, 146–147, 147, 154, 158, 159, 169
Clive Rose/Getty Images: 184–185
Vladimir Rys/Bongarts/Getty Images: 200
SSPL/Getty Images: 40
Rainer W. Schlegelmilch/Getty Images: 8–9, 54–55, 58–59, 60, 62–63, 64, 65, 66, 68–69, 72–73, 76, 78–79, 80–81, 82, 84, 85, 90, 98–99, 102, 108, 112–113, 114, 115, 116, 118, 119, 121, 124, 125, 128, 129, 132, 140, 144, 144–145, 151, 152, 152–153, 156–157, 162, 162–163, 164–165, 168–169, 170, 171, 173, 202–203
Ronald Startup/Getty Images: 30
The Cahier Archive/Corbis: 148–149
George Tiedemann/Corbis: 100, 103
Bob Thomas/Getty Images: 133
Mark Thompson/Allsport/Getty Images: 165, 186–187, 195
Tony Triolo/Sports Illustrated/Getty Images: 106
Universal /TempSport/Corbis: 23
Ted West/Getty Images: 50
J.Wilds/Stringer/Getty Images: 22
Witschel/Picture Alliance/IPA: 93
www.sutton-images.com: 48, 56, 70, 72, 91, 94, 96, 98, 104, 110, 122, 130, 134, 136
Zryzner/Shutterstock: 178–179

Published by Schiffer Publishing, Ltd.

4880 Lower Valley Road

Atglen, PA 19310

Phone: (610) 593-1777; Fax: (610) 593-2002

Email: info@schifferbooks.com

Web: www.schifferbooks.com

ISBN 978-0-7643-7063-2

Library of Congress Number: 2025935966

Printed in China

Cover Design: Jack Chappell

Piazzale Luigi Cadorna, 6
20123 Milan, Italy
www.whitestar.it

Updated edition

1 2 3 4 5 6   29 28 27 26 25